5/89

WHAT ARE THEY SAYING ABOUT
THE END OF THE WORLD?

What Are They Saying About the End of the World?

Zachary Hayes, O.F.M.

PAULIST PRESS
New York/Ramsey

The Publisher gratefully acknowledges use of material from J.A.T. Robinson's *In The End God* reprinted by permission of Harper & Row, Publishers, Inc.

Library of Congress
Catalog Card Number: 83-60372

ISBN: 0-8091-2550-1

Published by Paulist Press
545 Island Road, Ramsey, N.J. 07446

Printed and bound in the
United States of America

Contents

Preface

During my student years in Germany, I enjoyed the company of many colleagues blessed with a generous amount of Rhineland humor. Among the tales of German university life which they loved to tell was the story of a well-known professor of theology who lectured at length on the mysteries of Christian eschatology. This man had taken great care, so the story goes, to calculate the degrees of heat at the various levels of the other world which appeared to be structured much as it had been centuries before in Dante's *Divine Comedy*. The professor had solved many a difficult problem, but one question concerning the Last Judgment continued to elude him. Of what sort of metal would the trumpets of the Last Judgment be made? Here confessing his limitations, the good professor is reputed to have ended his lectures with a flourish: "We cannot determine whether the trumpets will be made of silver, of gold, or of brass. But one thing is certain. The trumpets will be blown!"

Put in those terms, the phenomenon of physical eschatology is revealed in its true nature. Who can hold back the smile that forces itself on us as we think of the theologian assuring us with proper solemnity that regardless of the metal involved, the great trumpets will indeed be blown? But even as we smile, we recognize in the story—which well may be apocryphal—the familiar sound of the sort of eschatology with which Roman Catholics were educated until very recent years. While the trumpets of the judgment day still resound with awesome power in the music of Verdi's *Requiem,* we hear less and less of them in religious instruction and in theology classrooms. Why is this the case?

Today theologians speak more about eschatology than they did twenty years ago. But they speak less about fire, worms, and trumpets and more about the life-giving power of God. The core of the Christian faith is found in the preaching of Jesus and in the resurrection of Jesus by God. But the promise implicit in Jesus' preaching and that of the resurrection cannot be said to have reached their full realization until they have been actualized in the entire body of the Lord. Faith in the resurrection of Christ includes hope in the consummation of the mystery anticipated in the resurrection. The eschatology implicit in the affirmation of the resurrection unfolds necessarily into an eschatology that is individual, collective, and cosmic.

From this perspective, eschatology is seen not as peripheral but as central to Christian faith. It expresses the ultimate dream that Christianity holds open to struggling humanity. In attempting to express this dream, the Christian Scriptures have used a wealth of symbols and metaphors the meaning of which cannot be reduced to precise definitions. Such images are more suggestive than informative. Taken as a whole, these symbols elicit an awareness of the future fulfillment of the mystery of Christ in the body of humanity and in the whole of the cosmos.

While styles of theology come and go, these metaphors and symbols have persisted over the generations. Yet different understandings of humanity and the world lead to different styles of interpreting these images. The style of a physical eschatology has given way to a style that is far more anthropological in tone. This change is one of the most basic factors in understanding why eschatology today sounds different than it did even in the very recent past.

This book is an attempt to provide a guide to the reader at two levels. First, it discusses the historical move from physical to anthropological eschatology with some of its implications. Second, it presents interpretations of the basic Christian eschatological symbols as they are understood by a number of influential theologians at the present time. In accord with the guidelines for this series, I have taken a consciously bibliographical approach but have attempted to organize the material within a systematic framework. At significant points in the presentation, I have allowed the authors to speak in their own words, particularly in cases where the pertinent sources are available only in German publications or in English editions that are not easily available to the ordinary reader.

This volume, with its emphasis on the collective aspect of eschatology, complements that of Monika Hellwig entitled *What Are They Saying About Death and Christian Hope?* which focused on the personal dimensions of eschatology. It relates also to my earlier volume in this series which was entitled *What Are They Saying About Creation?* There I attempted to draw out the connection between origins and finality in the doctrine of creation and closed the treatment with a brief statement on eschatology. The present volume can be seen as a companion piece which expands the seminal statement of the earlier work.

It is our hope that the materials discussed here will prove to be a welcome alternative to the style of eschatology that most often confronts us in the form of pessimistic, apocalyptic predictions of the end of the world that fills the shelves of our bookstores.

Abbreviations

DOGMA 6. Michael Schmaus, *Dogma VI: Justification and the Last Things*.

ESCH. Joseph Cardinal Ratzinger, *Eschatologie—Tod und Ewiges Leben. Kleine Katholische Dogmatik, IX*.

ENCYC. *Encyclopedia of Theology*.

IN THE END. J.A.T. Robinson, *In the End God*.

INTROD. Joseph Cardinal Ratzinger, *Introduction to Christianity*.

INVEST. Karl Rahner, *Theological Investigations*.

1
Recent History of Eschatology

Eschatology as it was commonly presented in the theological handbooks consisted almost totally in the well-known treatment of death, judgment, heaven, and hell. This material was treated as the final tract of dogmatic theology and commonly preached about at the end of retreats and parish missions. One could study all the other major tracts of theology and find virtually no reference to this matter. As Karl Barth remarked, eschatology became "a harmless little chapter at the end of dogmatic theology."[1]

Today theologians speak readily of the rediscovery of eschatology for Christian consciousness. This refers, first, to discoveries in the field of scriptural studies. One of the significant results of nineteenth and twentieth century exegetical work is the awareness that eschatological hopes are basic to the way revelation has taken place throughout a major portion of the Hebrew Scriptures. No less important is eschatological awareness for the Christian Easter proclamation and the Christian understanding of the life of Jesus of Nazareth. Eschatology is basic to the understanding of the Bible. This is not a fad but a solid result of critical studies which has yet to be adequately appropriated by systematic theology.

Early in this century, Karl Barth expressed his reaction to the discoveries of exegesis in the remark: "Christianity that is not thoroughly eschatological has absolutely nothing to do with Jesus Christ."[2] This fact, thought Barth, must have implications for every tract of theology. Roman Catholic reaction has been slower. Surveying the Catholic theological scene in the late 1950's, Hans Urs von Balthasar stated that it was possible to discern a wide variety of tendencies but no overall synthesis.[3] To a great extent his description remains applicable to the situation in Roman Catholic circles today. There is a variety of viewpoints but nothing even approaching an overall agreement.

The blame for this confusing situation cannot be laid only at the door of the systematicians. Scripture scholars themselves have been no less confused by their findings. While there is a widespread consensus among Catholic and Protestant exegetes that eschatology is basic to the biblical tradition, there is extensive disagreement on the precise nature and development of eschatology in both the Hebrew and the Christian Scriptures. Beyond this, there is little agreement as to how we should translate the concerns of biblical eschatology into categories congenial to contemporary thought.

Toward the end of the nineteenth century, the study of Johannes Weiss entitled *The Preaching of Jesus Concerning the Kingdom of God*[4] pulled the rug out from under nineteenth century Protestant liberal theology and set the stage for the future discussion of Christian eschatology as we find it even at the present time. Weiss argued that Christian Scriptures must be viewed in terms of their apocalyptic and eschatological nature. The kingdom of God, which is central to the preaching of Jesus, is not a new order which human beings could create in human society. On the contrary, it is always and totally God's gift to humanity breaking in from above in a great crisis. At the heart of Weiss' argument are two convictions: the kingdom is an act of God, and the kingdom as found in Jesus' preaching is a future reality. The foundation laid by Weiss was developed by Albert Schweitzer in the form of a thoroughly consistent *future* eschatology.[5] Jesus, according to Schweitzer, expected an imminent intervention of God that would end history and inaugurate a new age. Hence the urgency of his proclamation of God's Kingdom. Jesus' expectations were directed to the immediate future, and they were disappointed.

While the views of Weiss and Schweitzer are focused on texts that seem to speak in terms of the future, the interpretation of C.H. Dodd revolves around a different strand of the scriptural materials.[6] Because of the apparent emphasis on the intimate relation between the kingdom of God and the person and ministry of Jesus, Dodd argued that Jesus was not preaching about some future event but about what was happening in his own ministry. "The kingdom of God is among you" (Lk

17:21). The crisis of the kingdom is not to come in the future; it is present in Jesus' ministry. Confronted by Jesus, human persons undergo their judgment by the way in which they respond to him. This view has been called *realized* eschatology.

If, in the interpretation of Dodd, the eschatological language of Jesus' preaching seems to lose any significant reference to a temporal future, with Rudolf Bultmann the separation of chronology and eschatology is complete.[7] The *eschaton* is last not in a temporal sense but in a qualitative sense. It signifies that which is totally other. Eschatology does not speak of a future end of history. The meaning of history lies in the present. In every moment the possibility of eschatological meaning lies dormant. It must be awakened. Bultmann, with an obvious feeling of embarrassment at the language of the Christian Scriptures, makes use of Heideggerian philosophy to interpret the meaning of the mythical symbols that abound in Scripture. This style is called *existential* eschatology. It focuses on human meaning and ignores the cosmic dimensions of the Scriptures.

If each of the above seems inadequate because of the tendency to selectivity, the work of Oscar Cullmann is an attempt to deal more fully with the complexity of the scriptural material. As his view is elaborated in two studies,[8] it involves an understanding of *salvation history* which seems to do more justice to the scriptural data. In direct opposition to Bultmann, Cullmann argues that the eschatology of the Christian Scriptures must include chronology. The Scriptures reflect the Jewish concept of linear time punctuated by moments of unique redemptive significance. Jesus and his disciples were convinced that God's decisive saving action was taking place in Jesus' ministry. The appearance of Christ places a new division in the time-line which extends from creation to the parousia. This new division becomes the age of the Church and runs chronologically from the appearance of Christ to the parousia. Writing shortly after World War II, Cullmann formulates a metaphor from the war experience to express the tension which characterizes the time of the Church. He distinguished D-Day from VE-Day. The decisive battle has been won (D-Day = the life, death, resurrection of Christ), but the war must yet work itself out in cleaning-up exercises across Europe (VE-Day = the parousia of Christ, the end of history). This view seems to reflect both the present and the future dimensions of the scriptural language more adequately. But Cullmann's work is not without its own problems, and critics were quick to point them out. Does Cullmann really provide a satisfactory solution to the problem of the delayed parousia if we reflect on the fact that the delay has lasted more than nineteen hundred years already?

Cullmann's work can be seen as a critical response to the existential style of Bultmann. Another type of reaction to Bultmann can be traced to the appearance of Jürgen Moltmann's *Theology of Hope* in 1964.[9] Since Bultmann's style isolated Christian faith from questions about the meaning of world history, its inadequacy would inevitably be felt. Moltmann criticized Bultmann for the severe privatization of faith involved in the "eschatology of decision." For Moltmann, eschatology is not focused on the present, nor on a past "mid-point," nor on a lost eternity. Rather, it is focused on the *future*. Christian eschatology holds out a real future to humanity. But the future of eschatology stands in striking contrast with the present reality of the world. To hear the eschatological proclamation of the scriptures is to become aware of the contradiction between the present and the future. But this contradiction is not overcome merely by becoming conscious of it. Those who hear the eschatological message must respond by entering into the reality of the present world, upsetting it and contradicting it so as to bring it beyond its present condition. For Christians, eschatological preaching is a summons to participate in the pain of a suffering Messiah in the effort to bring about not only a new level of human consciousness but a new reality for the world.

It seems clear that this style of *political* eschatology sees the Gospel as a summons to political involvement of a revolutionary sort. If the relation between present and future is one of contradiction, one moves to the future by the upheaval of the present. When that dialectic is translated into political terms, it lends itself to a most revolutionary interpretation. While this style of eschatology offers a way out of the narcissism of existentialism, it brings with it its own problems and dangers. Is it really a legitimate procedure to transform Christian eschatology into political utopias? There seems to be little basis in Scripture for viewing the kingdom of God as a directly political concept that could have direct relevance as a political norm. One must ask whether this entire procedure does not, ultimately, transform the Christian Gospel into yet another ideology of the future.

The privatization of Christianity to which Moltmann objected found another critic in Johann Baptist Metz, a Roman Catholic who develops his thought in the form of a *Theology of the World.*[10] After doing his doctoral studies under Karl Rahner, Metz emerged as a proponent of a style that is intended to transcend the non-historical, metaphysical style of theology dominant in Roman Catholic thought until recently. In place of an archaic relation to the past, Metz urges a functional relation to the future. This is called for, he argues, because of the basic change in our relation to the world. We no longer encounter the world as "charged with the grandeur of God" but as made over into a world of human meaning. The world has become a humanly-made world, and our relation to it has become far more active than contemplative. Contemporary religious consciousness encounters God not so much in objects as in human hope for the future. In order to meet this hope, Christianity needs a theology which is based on biblical eschatology and has a critical, social orientation. Such a theology would provide a basis for the critique of ideologies and social structures that become absolutized. Thus theology would serve to hold human history open to its ultimate future with God. Metz's theology of the world is not a theology of the cosmos, nor of the transcendental orientation of the individual person, but a theology of the emerging political and social order. In this sense, it is *political* theology.

While the early reflections of both Moltmann and Metz reflected much of the humanistic optimism of the 1960's in the call for a Christianity engaged in the social process, their thought took on a new coloration with the sense of disillusionment that swept through the ranks of the idealists in Europe and North America. Without repudiating the *Theology of Hope,* Moltmann developed his dialectic of contradiction more systematically in the elaborate treatment given to the theology of the cross.[11]

Here the sense of human tragedy is strong. We are called upon to hope in freedom in spite of suffering. While Metz seemed in his early work to be quite optimistic in his expectations of what human beings would do to move the world to a new and better future, some years later he would underscore human history as a history of suffering which "unites all men like a 'second nature.'"[12]

Among German theologians, a controversial position on specific eschatological symbols was taken by Gisbert Greshake and Gerhard Lohfink.[13] Their view focuses strongly on the meaning of such symbols as the resurrection of the dead and the second coming of Christ. They argue for the resurrection of each individual immediately in death. Eschatology, they claim, has no reference to a final point of linear time; the parousia cannot mean that God will appear in his unveiled reality to the final generation of human history. On the contrary, the parousia is taking place at each moment when a human person dies and appears before God. Thus, they see no need to speak of an interim state between individual death and general resurrection.

Joseph (now Cardinal) Ratzinger attempted a critical answer to this development in his *Eschatologie: Tod und ewiges Leben.*[14] Ratzinger concentrates strongly on the relation between eschatology and anthropology, arguing for a distinctively Christian concept of the soul and for a duality but not a dualism in the understanding of the human person. From this anthropological basis, he criticizes those views which fail to take adequate account of both the spiritual and the bodily dimensions of the human person. He argues emphatically for a distinction between individual and general resurrection and for an end of history as we now experience it.

Two years later, Herbert Vorgrimler published a monograph, *Hoffnung auf Vollendung,* which provides a handy summary of the state of the question together with a constructive statement of his own.[15] Vorgrimler's presentation is sympathetic to the word of Greshake and Lohfink and reflects a heavy influence of Karl Rahner's theology of death.

The work of Moltmann and Metz in Europe has provided inspiration for the development of a variety of theologies of praxis in Latin America, including the work of Leonardo Boff, Gustavo Gutiérrez, and Juan Luis Segundo.[16] While these and numerous other authors are commonly referred to as liberation theologians, this designation is deceptive since it readily creates the impression of a commonly accepted body of teaching. In fact, what these authors share is not so much a body of doctrine as the attempt to develop theology from participation in the process of liberation. They differ significantly in the manner in which they carry out this project. The foundational significance of biblical eschatology plays a major role together with the emphasis on social criticism and the call to *praxis* as a means of achieving not only an authentic consciousness but a new reality in the political and social order.

It is not surprising, therefore, to find that the biblical metaphor of the kingdom of God plays a crucial role in the eschatology of praxis theologians. Most of these authors reject the exclusively existential eschatology of Bultmann and other European theologians, preferring to see the kingdom as a metaphor which makes possible a link between faith and social-political reality. Precisely in working out this link, praxis theologians differ greatly among themselves. But the attempt to construct the link commonly reflects some sort of social-political analysis from the viewpoint of the particular form of oppression that provides the concrete point of departure for theological reflection. While the kingdom elicits the awareness of a future beyond history, that future— for praxis theologians—is not unrelated to the process of history and to the structure of society.

This survey of the development of eschatological styles since the beginning of the twentieth century is by no means complete. My intention is merely to point out some of the major stepping stones along the way. From the retrieval of biblical eschatology as a basic datum of modern exegesis, we have seen a variety of attempts to deal with the larger implications of this datum. It becomes clear that the word "eschatology" for current Christian thought is like a code word that conjures up a cluster of very difficult questions never envisioned in the classical tract "on the last things." Above all, we discover a growing tendency to move from eschatology as the concern for personal meaning to eschatology as the question of the final destiny of the human race and the world. With this comes a significant shift to the relation of Christian faith to social and political process, for this area of human activity is crucial in whatever future the world may have. If the future of which Christianity speaks is a future given by God as pure grace, what is the relation between that future and all the activity by which human beings attempt to create a future for themselves in the world?

Von Balthasar had spoken of a variety of tendencies in eschatology. Though he said this in 1957, it remains an apt description of the situation today. In the light of that variety and of the fundamental place of eschatology in Christian faith, it becomes important to attempt to draw up some guidelines for assessing and interpreting eschatological statements. If these statements can mean anything we choose, then they really have no meaning.

2
From Physics to Anthropology

Signs of Change

The reflections of the previous chapter show that theology today is inclined not to think of eschatology as detailed information about future events at the end of the world. Nor is it concerned with giving a vivid description of the "next world." Instead, it tends to approach eschatology as reflection on the fulfillment of what God's creative power brings about in humanity and in the world.

The signs of this shift in general orientation can be seen in two early essays, one by Yves Congar and one by Hans Urs von Balthasar.[1] Congar decries the theological style of the handbooks which had treated eschatology as an accumulation of "things" that follow death, things that could be studied with the same methods by which one studies earthly objects. "One asks 'What is the fire of purgatory? Is the vision of God through an intelligible species?' and the questions are posed in the same way as those about the essence of fire in physics or the meaning of conceptual knowledge in epistemology. In short, we have tried to answer eschatological questions with the methods of natural knowledge." Congar calls this a physical style of eschatology and sees it to be in sharp contrast with eschatology as found in Scripture and in the Fathers of the Church where eschatology points to the essential meaning of history, to that which constitutes the inner ferment of the entire present order, a mystery that will be fully revealed only in its final outcome.

12

Echoing the same concerns in the late 1950's, Von Balthasar points out that the sheer extent of the universe and its history as known to the modern mind renders it a hopeless task "to think of locating the eschatological 'places' (heaven, hell, purgatory, limbo) within the limit of one world—to do so would make a physical universe out of a theological cosmos." Against this background, Von Balthasar describes a shift or a reduction in eschatology to what appears to be the decisive issue in revelation: "an immediate relating of the creature to God alone, who becomes, in place of 'things' and 'states,' the creature's Last Thing." This biblical hope is expressed in Psalm 72: "Yet with you I shall always be. Whom else have I in heaven? But for me, to be near God is my good." Similarly, St. Augustine writes: "After this life, God himself is our place" (*Enarrat. in Ps. XXX, serm.* III, n. 8). Von Balthasar paraphrases Augustine in the following: "God is the Last Thing of the creature. Gained, He is its paradise; lost, He is its hell; as demanding, He is its judgment; as cleansing, He is its purgatory." In such a formulation, eschatology has been reduced to a statement focused on the final relation between God and his creation.

In a more specifically Christological sense, writes Jean Daniélou, the ultimate relation of creation with God is that which has been realized in the mystery of Christ.[2] He is the eschaton, the end of all things; for Christian faith believes that in Jesus Christ God has revealed himself as the salvation of humankind. Here, the reduction is focused clearly on the person and destiny of Jesus insofar as he realizes and reveals the ultimate fulfillment of creation in the presence of God. This shift clarifies why it is that eschatology cannot be clear and distinct knowledge. One cannot treat the ultimate mystery of a personal God and of the creature's relation to a personal God as though this were a "knowable object" without distorting the meaning of faith as a loving, trusting surrender of the person to the personal truth of God.

Von Balthasar's description of this reduction is followed by the sketch of an expansion; for the Christological reduction must be worked out in its implications for the whole of theology. This development, says Von Balthasar, is only beginning and must eventually be worked out in relation to the doctrine of creation, salvation, ecclesiology, sacramentology, and the theology of history. Von Balthasar singles out Michael Schmaus as one who has recognized this need and who has begun to give theology a new face from the perspective of eschatology.

Principles and Criteria

If, as Von Balthasar maintains, eschatology is the "storm center" of contemporary theology, we cannot look at the present situation without asking whether there are guidelines to help us along the way. It is one thing to know that eschatology is basic to Scripture and Christian faith; it is quite another thing to know what to do with this fact. How are we to understand the puzzling history of eschatological development in the Bible? How are we to interpret the confusing language of apocalyptic in the Scriptures? How does all this bear on our understanding of Jesus Christ? If we stand at the center of a storm, we are well advised to look for a rope to hold onto lest we be swept off the deck.

Lutheran theologian Carl Braaten offers four criteria for making appropriate eschatological statements.[3] The first two criteria represent the need to be true to the biblical witness on the one side and to relate this witness to present human experience on the other side. Thus, eschatological statements should be *existentially relevant* and controlled by the *kerygma* deriving from Scripture. The second two criteria are more specifically related to the mystery of Christ. Here Braaten holds that eschatological statements must be *centered on Christ* as the eschaton, and *futuristic,* or concerned with that realm of hope which comes from God's victory in the resurrection of Christ. As criteria, these remain rather formal and abstract, but they do—in their own way—reflect the kind of theistic and Christological reduction described by Von Balthasar.

Karl Rahner has treated the question of interpretation in an essay that has been widely influential, especially among Catholics.[4] Rahner's fundamental principle is a clear statement of the Christological reduction. "Eschatology is a forward look which is necessary to man for his spiritual decision in freedom, and it is made from the standpoint of his situation in saving history as this is determined by the Christ Event." For Rahner, our present experience of faith and grace is already an eschatological situation, though it is one that is characterized by incompleteness and hence contains within itself the dynamism of a projection of future completion and fulfillment. This means that eschatological knowledge is not clear conceptual knowledge about future events or objects, but an obscure expectation of the possible fulfillment of the grace experienced already now in the present. Since the eschatological future depends ultimately on the radical self-gift of God to his creatures, it remains always an uncontrollable mystery. Precisely because it is incalculable, it is the condition for the decisive exercise of human freedom. We can relate to such a future appropriately only by hope, trust, and radical surrender of ourselves.

The key insight of Rahner's principle is this: Christian eschatology is not a preview of the end of the world or of the structure of the "next" world. Rather, it is a form of projection or extrapolation from the Christian experience of the present into the mode of future fulfillment. Some further implications of this in the form of subsidiary principles will be discussed later in this chapter. This basic principle reflects the central role which Christ plays throughout Rahner's thought, and it is rooted in the transcendental anthropology which is so fundamental to his system. The convergence of Christology and anthropology allows for a form of eschatology of impressive interpretative power.

Christian Schütz singles out four criteria which strongly reflect the influence of Rahner's essay.[5] Corresponding to the foundational significance of the Gospel and its forward-looking, prophetic dynamism, the first criterion emphasizes that eschatological statements must have an appropriate relationship to the Gospel. In line with the hermeneutic circle commonly recognized today, this evangelical criterion is juxtaposed with a second which singles out the present experience of the believer. Any eschatological statement which in principle is closed to that experience is questionable. As a third criterion, Schütz says that eschatological statements should let the future be a true future. Future and present should not be merged. Future is not-yet. But the future emerges out of present reality, though its precise form is not predictable and not knowable. Finally, eschatological statements should allow us to distinguish between God, humanity, and the world, and to leave to God that future which is not ours to create or confer. Experimental, scientific knowledge and planning for the future is a prerogative of humanity. But the truly eschatological future is reserved to God and cannot be formulated or contained in human programs of world-formation.

Edward Schillebeeckx situates his approach to eschatological interpretation in the larger context of his understanding of the historical development of future-consciousness in the Bible. "Because Israel remembered certain meaningful events from the past and associated them with new events of the present, both past and present illuminated each other,

and thus it experienced and interpreted its history as the gradual fulfillment of a divine promise." It is in this context of "a critically examined
history of traditions" that we come to understand the dynamic of *promise* with its openness to the future and its "definitive fulfillment in Jesus
Christ."[6]

From this perspective, Schillebeeckx comes to an agreement with
Rahner: "The Bible gives no anticipating historical report over the
eschaton. We know nothing about the transcendent ultimate things—
judgment, Christ's return, heaven, hell, purgatory—except insofar as
they are already indicated in the course of historical events expressing
the actual relationship between the God of the covenant and mankind,
particularly in Christ, 'the last Adam'—i.e. 'the man of the
eschaton.'"[7] In his own way, he reflects Rahner's view that eschatology is speech about the future from out of present Christian experience.
"Eschatology is the expression of the belief that history is in God's
hands, that the history of the world *can* reach its fulfillment in communion with God and that it *will* be brought to this fulfillment in Christ who
embodies God's promise."[8]

Other Aspects of Eschatology

1. *Hope as a Human Phenomenon.* In the 1960's, especially in
Europe, attempts were made at serious dialogue between Christians and
Marxists. Because of the nature of Marxist philosophy, much of the
discussion involved questions of eschatology and anthropology. Marxist philosopher Ernst Bloch[9] was a significant figure in these
discussions. The influence of his phenomenological studies of human
hope can be seen in the explicit emphasis given to the anthropological
roots of hope in a wide range of Christian theologians. Rahner's style
would incline him in this direction independently of any contact with
Marxism. But the presence of this theme in Pannenberg, Moltmann,
and more recently in John Macquarrie's *Christian Hope* shows clear evidence of the influence of Bloch's work.[10] To the extent that we can
locate a fundamentally human basis for the language of hope, the possibility of interpreting human experience through the language of biblical
eschatology becomes more actual. Biblical eschatology expresses a certain kind of hope. But if hope emerges from hidden depths of human

experience, then the symbols and metaphors of the Bible suggest a way of articulating and interpreting human hope.

Bloch's philosophical analysis may be seen as a highly refined and nuanced development of Marx's dictum that religion is the "opium of the people." For Bloch, humanity is incomplete in its concrete existence and alienated from its essence which lies in the future. From out of the tension between existence and essence, humanity projects itself into its future in the effort to realize its own essence. It is this impulse that provides the basis of all the language of hope. It is in religion that the essence of humanity finds its fullest expression, specifically in the eschatological language of the Scriptures. The real substratum underlying all religions is "hope in its totality." Bloch argues further that not only is religion the fullest expression of the essence of humanity, but Christianity is the appearance of the real essence of religion. Following that line of reasoning, we can conclude that the truest expression of what it means to be human is given in Christianity. What impresses Bloch about the Bible is its dynamic, eschatological messianism. This can sound very attractive to Christians up to this point. But Bloch continues by saying that hope can lead to two very different forms of reaction. On the one hand, it can lead to resignation and passivity. On the other hand, it can lead to active, aggressive efforts to change the world. The trouble with historic Christianity, writes Bloch, is that Christians have been too readily inclined to the first route and have allowed their hope to turn them from this world to the next.

This analysis has left its mark on Pannenberg and Moltmann. What is important for both of them is that Bloch's analysis provides a human point of contact for the biblical promise of the kingdom of God. Braaten writes that "Bloch's philosophy of hope is being hailed as a secular confirmation of the fact that biblical eschatology deals with what is central in human existence; man's hopes burst open his present, connect him with his past, drive him toward the horizons of the not yet realized future."[11] Bloch has shown as few others the power of an open future for human life; he allows Christians to become serious once more about something basic to their own religious tradition. It is in the light of the future that Pannenberg attempts to reformulate the understanding of metaphysics. Like Bloch, Pannenberg speaks of the "pull of the future." God is the "power of the future." It is not so much the present that causes the future, but the future that causes the present, pulling humanity like a mighty magnet out of a secure present into an uncertain future.

Reflecting Bloch, Macquarrie argues that we must first understand hope as a human phenomenon so that "we shall be conscious of how [Christian hope] is related to all the other hopes of the human race, and we shall be less likely to fall into that widespread error of separating it off as a highly peculiar kind of hope, having little or nothing to do with the hopes that belong to our everyday life in the world" (*Christian Hope,* p. 2). Macquarrie distinguishes between hope and total hope. This distinction is similar to Rahner's distinction between categorical and absolute hope. Both Macquarrie and Rahner begin by pointing out how human beings are creatures of hope in very ordinary levels of experience. On a day-to-day basis we express our hope in the many tasks and projects and plans through which we attempt to work out the meaning of our lives. For both Macquarrie and Rahner, hope is the driving power that undergirds the unfolding of humanity in a temporal process. The full meaning of our human present is realized through the appropriation of our past as it continues to live in our present, and through the projections into the future whereby one hopes to bring to fulfillment the promise contained already in the present. Thus, hope expresses the dynamism of the incomplete human being as it projects itself to the future in a quest for meaning.

But this raises the question of the limits of human hope. Our "little" hopes can be understood, first of all, in terms of a very specific cultural context which places limits on what we can hope for. Though contexts can shift and expand, they remain specific contexts that place particular limits on human hope. Yet we continue to hope. The ultimate limit to hope which we must face is death. The human question of meaning seems never to be decisively answered in history. Thus arises the truly eschatological question: What can we hope for in the face of death? As Rahner sees it, the eschatological question is not whether some part or dimension of our humanity can find fulfillment, but whether there is fulfillment for our being as such. Macquarrie has the same issue in mind when he speaks of total hope. Total hope "is hope that reaches out beyond particular situations of hoping to embrace life as a whole—the life of an individual or even the life of a community or of the whole human race. It may even be possible to conceive of a hope for the world itself" (*Christian Hope,* p. 18).

This anthropological turn in current theology reflects a significant influence of the Christian-Marxist dialogue. When it is carried out well, it need not lead to any humanistic reductionism. It helps us locate the appropriate dimension of human experience to which Christian eschatological language addresses itself.

2. *Symbols and Metaphors.* The anthropological orientation described above has led to a fuller awareness of the nature and function of eschatological language. Congar had already pointed out that eschatological "knowledge" is not like knowledge of ordinary objects. If by "knowledge" we refer to the common intellectual processes of defining, arguing, deducing, and judging, it might be more accurate to say we do not "know" eschatological realities. While it is possible to use the term "knowledge" to refer analogically to a wide range of human experiences, it can be misleading to speak of our intimations of the future as "knowledge."

It might be helpful to distinguish "knowing" from "hoping." If knowledge is expressed in defining, articulating, and judging, hope is expressed in pictures and images. Hope does not close things but holds them open. It sees reality not only as it is but as it is capable of changing for the better. Hope expresses itself in pictures, dreams, and symbols which point to what lies beyond knowledge. Of all the areas of theological language, that of eschatology is understandably the most emphatically symbolic and metaphorical.

What is the function of such language? It is certainly not to provide clear information about future world-events (e.g., destruction of the world) or of extra-terrestrial places (heaven, hell, purgatory). Yet it does have an important positive function. The symbols and metaphors of eschatology make us consciously aware of and therefore open to the mystery which lies beyond our power to comprehend or to control. Precisely because they make us more aware of mystery, writes Rahner, they open up the realm in which human freedom can operate. We know the future "as something blissfully incomprehensible which is accepted in freedom and therefore in danger of being lost" (*Encyc.*, p. 437).

3. *Eschatology and Apocalyptic.* In formulating his basic principle for interpreting eschatological statements, Rahner emphasizes the fact that such a principle makes it possible to distinguish eschatology from "false apocalyptic." Rahner has formulated the difference as follows. Eschatology is extrapolation from the Christian present into the future; apocalyptic is interpolation from the future into the present. Some comments about this are necessary.

Of all that Rahner has suggested thus far, this distinction is probably the most debatable among scholars. On the one hand, there is a vast body of serious religious literature which is commonly referred to as apocalyptic literature. On the other hand, there are many people who seem to do precisely what Rahner describes. The many books of Hal Lindsey provide a clear case. Whether one is justified in explaining this extensive religious apocalyptic literature by the same dynamism that seems to be operative in popular, science-fiction apocalyptic is the question. It is quite possible, for example, to interpret the apocalyptic material as a specific form of eschatology emerging out of the same basic dynamic that undergirds eschatology. Rahner's language is confusing. It is possible to use the term "apocalyptic" for that style of literature that focuses on the physical cataclysm that will bring our world to a stunning, final conflagration. The authors of this literature commonly speculate about the nations that will be involved and the date of the end. Rahner makes it possible to distinguish serious Christian eschatology from this sort of literature. But that does not give a full account of religious apocalyptic literature which, among other things, includes a rich theology of history and of creation. This is not adequately dealt with simply as "interpolation from the future into the present." It represents factors that should be a concern for serious theology.

In this chapter we have sketched the basic shifts in eschatological reflection: from physical eschatology to a focus on Christology and anthropology. This shift makes it possible to see new dimensions of meaning in eschatological language. While many favorite views are lost in the process, this shift offers new and unsuspected riches to those who attempt to travel this road.

3
Dimensions of Eschatology

Individual and Collective Eschatology

The style of eschatological preaching with which we are most familiar has tended to emphasize the destiny of the individual person. This is understandable both from the perspective of the individual believer and from that of the preacher. It is easy to understand that a person will be concerned about his or her personal destiny. What happens to a person who dies? Is death painful? Is death an annihilation? Does something await the person beyond death? The increasing interest in death and dying in recent years is a symptom of how deeply this kind of concern is embedded in human consciousness.

The emphasis given to these questions of individual eschatology may easily create the impression that these are the primary and perhaps the only significant questions for Christian eschatology. Such a conclusion would be serious distortion. Indeed, as the historical development of the future-consciousness of the Jewish people indicates, the first concern was the collective future, the future of the people. It was relatively late in the history of the Hebrew Scriptures that the question of the destiny of the individual emerged explicitly. How would the faithful individual share in the fulfillment of the divine promise? Similarly, in the Christian Scriptures and in patristic theology, the primary frame of reference for eschatology is the collective, the *totus Christus* of St. Augustine. One looks forward to the restoration of the unity of the human race united as one body with its head, Jesus Christ. This does not exclude the question of the individual but situates it within the collective.

Recent eschatological studies have shifted away from an exclusive concern for individual eschatology to a renewed sense of the collective. The new awareness of Scripture and of the Fathers has contributed to this shift to questions about the future of the Church, the human race, and the world.

Moltmann pointed out in his *Theology of Hope* that the question of the human future is not asked fully until it is raised with respect to the individual and the collective future in the face of death. Though the individual dimension is not adequately developed in his work, we could conclude that, in principle, eschatology should include both the individual and the collective. It must deal not only with the future of the human race, but also with the way in which the individual can hope to participate in that future. Unless eschatology deals with the latter, it will become a mere ideology of the future in which the present and the individual become mere steps to the future.

Rahner has developed these issues more fully and in an explicitly Christian way on the basis of his fundamental principle. Since that principle turns our attention to the mystery of Christ, eschatology is a working out of a series of analogical implications of the Christ-mystery. In the present case, eschatology reflects on two dimensions of Christology. First, the teaching of the Church about Christ is concerned with an individual human being, Jesus of Nazareth, and with his life, death and ultimate destiny. If that individual human history and destiny provides the clues for understanding our ultimate relation with God, then there must be an individual eschatology. Second, the proclamation of Jesus' resurrection is a proclamation that the collective destiny of the human race and, indeed, of the world has been definitively decided and begun in him. Therefore, there must be a collective eschatology. Both the individual and the collective are essential to Christian teaching. "Eschatology can never sacrifice one to the other" (*Encyc.*, p. 435).

Reflecting this renewed sense of the collective dimension, many theologians place the primary emphasis there and attempt to reflect on the individual destiny only with the context of the collective. Thus, the fifth edition of Schmaus' *Katholische Dogmatik* (IV, 2) deals first with the typical questions of collective or general eschatology. These include the kingdom of God, the parousia of Christ, the resurrection of the dead, the general judgment, and the "new heaven and the new earth." Schmaus' treatment is strongly Christological and Trinitarian in tone.

The final state of the world is seen by way of extrapolation from the transforming mystery of Christ's resurrection. It is only against the background of this general eschatology that Schmaus takes up the characteristic themes of individual eschatology. The more recent text of Schmaus' English work *Dogma* reflects the same basic orientation but includes some further reflections in the light of Teilhard and of the Marxist-Christian dialogues.

A similar emphasis is found in Macquarrie's *Christian Hope* (pp. 107ff.) where the problem of individual eschatology is taken up in the final fifteen pages of the book. Macquarrie readily admits that it is easier for him to deal with the collective dimension. While recognizing the importance of the individual, Macquarrie seems to be influenced by the British analyst problem with the possibility of conceptualizing an after-life for the individual. While he is not willing to give up the idea, he presents a formulation which seems close to process theology's concept of immortality in the memory of God. While Macquarrie's position seems more subtle than the usual process view, it still remains unclear and problematic.

Spirit and Matter

Recent eschatology reflects a paradoxical pendulum movement. Not too long ago, theologians were quite content to speak of the immortality of the soul. In the light of more recent biblical research emphasizing a more holistic anthropology and a more concrete eschatology, many theologians criticized the notion of an immortal soul as an unfortunate Hellenization. A more biblical view, so it was felt, would emphasize the resurrection of the body and the salvation of the whole person in all the dimensions of its being. However, to deal with the obvious embarrassment of an excessively crude view of resurrection, it was felt necessary to spiritualize the notion of resurrection so that it became hardly distinguishable from the notion of the soul from which the discussion took its point of departure.

This is said not in a cynical sense, but in the hope that it might highlight a problem for Christian eschatology. There is ample evidence that the biblical eschatological hopes are, indeed, hopes for the whole of human existence. Biblical anthropology often seems more holistic than Hellenistic anthropology. Yet biblical anthropology recognizes a plurality of dimensions in human existence such as flesh, soul, and spirit. It is important, furthermore, that there are developments of anthropology in the Bible that seem remarkably close to Greek anthropology. A simple appeal to biblical anthropology does not solve the problems concerning the eschatological destiny of the "whole human person."

As a systematician, Rahner points out the unity and multiplicity that characterize human existence when it is viewed philosophically. Within a fundamental unity there are many dimensions that cannot be reduced one to the other. For Rahner, the eschatological question is the question of the fulfillment of human existence as such—whether our existence must "attain salvation in all its dimensions" (*Encyc.*, p. 437). There is no *a priori* reason for excluding any dimension of human nature from eschatology.

For Rahner, a phenomenology of human experience reveals, among other polarities, that of matter and spirit within a unity of being. Both matter and spirit—as principles of human existence in the world—must be dealt with in eschatology in dialectical statements concerning the "beatitude of the soul" and the "resurrection of the body." This flows consistently from Rahner's view that eschatological statements refer to the "unified human person in his totality" (*Invest.* 4, p. 331). In this regard, Rahner's principles seem more adequate to the theological tradition and to a philosophical phenomenology than do those views which so spiritualize resurrection that eschatology makes no statements whatever about materiality. Rahner firmly rejects all such views as forms of "Platonizing" eschatology.

In a similar vein and reflecting insights of Aquinas, Rahner, and Teilhard, Ratzinger argues against all attempts to exclude materiality from ultimate fulfillment. He concludes: "What the new world will be like cannot be conceptualized. Nor are there any concrete statements about the nature of humanity's relation to materiality in the new world and about the 'body of the resurrection' from which to form any conception. But we are certain that the dynamism of the cosmos is oriented to a goal, to a situation in which matter and spirit will be related to each other in a new and definitive way. This certainty remains the concrete content of the confession of the resurrection of the flesh even today; indeed, especially today"(*Esch.*, p. 160).

Ratzinger's view reflects the influence of the idealistic philosophies of history. Such religious symbols as the "Last Day," the "end of the world," and the "resurrection of the flesh" are symbols of the end of the total historical process (*Esch.*, p. 158). Since from the time of Kant and Hegel one can hardly envision the historical process except in terms of the ultimate unification of the multiple dimensions of the historical dialectic, Ratzinger concludes that a situation in which matter and spirit would stand in static juxtaposition would contradict the essential meaning of history, of creation, and of the very word of the Bible. The *eschaton* is the fulfillment of the whole, not merely of a part.

Echoing a similar concern about materiality, Schmaus argues more specifically from his understanding of the risen Christ: "Must the world somehow be explained in terms of the risen Christ?" (*Dogma* 6, p. 211). Genesis 2–3 and Romans 8 suggest that the destiny of the world is intertwined with that of humanity. Schmaus suggests an approach through an understanding of evolution derived from Teilhard and modified by Rahner's dialectical view of matter and spirit. Evolution is not explained in terms of matter alone, but in terms of matter interacting with its ground. Each stage of history includes an "action from above" and a "movement from below." Materiality is ultimately open to the transforming presence of God. Without becoming more specific, Schmaus concludes: "The thought is not fantastic that matter might attain a mode of existence similar to that of the glorified Christ and of humanity gathered into unity in Him" (*Dogma* 6, p. 213).

Difficult as the question may be, the materiality of human existence is an unavoidable issue for Christian eschatology. Precisely the appeal to the Bible raises the question with insistence, and the materialistic philosophies so dominant in the contemporary Western world point to the importance of a *theological* understanding of materiality. Christian faith may not give clear and specific answers to the fundamental nature of matter and spirit, but—if taken seriously—it will hold us open to serious thought about the nature of the world in which we live.

Eschatology and Other Theological Tracts

It has been suggested earlier in our presentation that the modern rediscovery of eschatology must eventually be worked out in terms of its implications for the other areas of theology. This task is as yet hardly begun, but some developments have been made.

1. *God*. In his *Theology of Hope,* Moltmann questioned the long-standing tendency to conceptualize God in terms of the classical metaphysics of being. Both Moltmann and Pannenberg have suggested the possibility that if the biblical experience of promise were pushed to its metaphysical implications, we might be challenged with alternate modes of conceptualizing God. This is reflected in the tendency to speak of divine transcendence in the language of the future. For Pannenberg, God reveals himself from the standpoint of the end of history. God is humanity's "not-yet." Like Bloch, Pannenberg speaks of God as the "pull of the future," the "power of the future," our "ultimate future." In an attempt to develop the metaphysical implications of biblical eschatology, Pannenberg speaks of a reversal of causes. Instead of thinking that the present causes the future, we are asked to say that the future causes the present. God as our future is a magnet drawing us from the stability of the present into an unknown future which ultimately is God himself.

2. *Creation*. The relation between creation and eschatology first emerged in biblical studies. In speaking of eschatology, both the Hebrew and the Christian Scriptures frequently employ the language of creation. Thus the fulfillment of the world is seen as a "new creation," a "new heaven and earth." The redemptive work of Christ is described as the creation of the "new Adam" or the "final Adam." Eschatological themes and symbols are obvious throughout the opening chapters of Genesis. The parallels between the garden of Genesis and the eschatological dreams of the prophets are clear.

From a systematic perspective, we find the tendency to see God's act of creation as an act that "places the possibility of the end" (L. Scheffczyk, A. Hulsbosch, M. Schmaus, J. Auer). The eschatological question, on the other hand, is the question of the fulfillment of what is begun in creation. Thus, one sees an intrinsic relation between the act of creation and the act of consummation. The world that flows from the act of creation is not only finite but incomplete. It is placed in an historical movement toward its God-intended completion. The elements of its history are complex (nature-grace, sin-redemption, etc.), and the movement of history is not a mechanical process since it hinges on the exercise of human freedom. But the world of God's creation never really exists independently of its orientation to fulfillment in God. For this reason, when the intrinsic relation between creation and eschatology has been recognized, it becomes necessary to redefine the categories of nature and grace so as to show more convincingly how grace can truly be the perfection of nature without either destroying nature or being extrinsic to it.

3. *Christology and Ecclesiology*. More than any other area of theology, that of Christology has been reshaped in a major way by eschatology. This in turn has basic implications for the doctrine on the Church. The awareness of the eschatological nature of the preaching and ministry of Jesus has provided the impulse behind the many new attempts to develop the theological significance of the life of Jesus as an integral component of Christology. The ministry of Jesus and his death and resurrection are approached within the context of eschatology and apocalyptic and yield the basic clues as to the nature of God and of his manner of acting in the world. On the other hand, when the Christ-mystery is viewed precisely as the eschatological fulfillment of the world in a human being, it yields crucial insights into the nature of the world and of humanity (K. Rahner, W. Kasper, E. Schillebeeckx, L. Boff, J. Sobrino).

If the starting point of Christology is inaccessible except by way of eschatology, this is laden with implications about the origin and nature of the Church and its structures. (H. Küng, R. McBrien, A. Dulles, *Lumen gentium*). Thus, recent ecclesiology reflects the implications of saying that Christ came above all to preach the kingdom of God. Why we have a Church and what relation the Church has to Christ and the kingdom are difficult questions. But any answer to them today reflects a deeper awareness of the role that human beings have played in developing Church structures and doctrines. The treatment of the Church's mission can no longer overlook the fact that the Church is not to be identified with the kingdom of God. Loisy may have overstated the case when he said: "Jesus preached the kingdom and what came to be is the Church," but the Church was not the object of Jesus' preaching. The mission of the Church is derived from its nature as an instrument of the kingdom. Since the full realization of the kingdom is to be found in a future relation between God and the world, the Church must be the opponent of all things in itself and in society that stand in the way of the realization of that relationship. Thus, ecclesiology under the power of eschatology tends to emphasize the role of the Church as critic not only of itself but of society at large (Moltmann, Pannenberg, Metz).

With this, we have touched on some of the basic dimensions of eschatology as they are reflected in theology today. It is clear that when one begins to reflect systematically on the theological meaning of the "rediscovery" of eschatology, the implications reach far beyond the rewriting of the classical tract on death, judgment, heaven, and hell. Indeed, we are confronted with questions that reach into all major areas of theology.

4
History and the
Future of the World

History and the Future

The current literature of futurology reflects an interest in the future which human beings may create for themselves. The future does not simply happen to us; it is something we actively bring about, at least in part. The Christian faith holds open to humanity a future and sees that future to be conferred ultimately by God as the fulfillment of his grace. The basic Christian claim about the future is contained in the confession of the resurrection of Christ by which the Christian community proclaims that God has acted decisively in Jesus and thus has opened our future to us. Christian eschatology, then, by its very nature raises the question of the relation between this ultimate self-gift of God to his creation on the one hand and the historical work of humanity on the other. If eschatology deals with the definitive state of salvation, and if that is ultimately the pure self-gift of God, what possible meaning can we see in human work to create a future in the world? Are our efforts to build a better world on earth really related to the "coming of the kingdom of God"? Or do we simply leave all we have done behind in death like an empty husk?

This question has emerged in recent decades with particular force. It was the concern of various forms of incarnationalism in the 1950's and 1960's. Incarnationalists could take their inspiration from the ecclesiology of nineteenth century Tübingen theologian Johann Möhler.

Stressing the doctrine of the Church as an extension of the incarnation through space and time, incarnationalists are inclined to say that by the mystery of the incarnation, Christ summons us to make this world an anticipation of the kingdom, at least to some degree. As represented in the writings of Henri de Lubac, Teilhard de Chardin, Gustav Thils, Walter Ong, and Christopher Butler, incarnationalism is inclined to emphasize the need of a genuine Christian humanism. Characteristic of this view is a concern for Christian engagement in the world. Focusing their concern on Christ in his life and ministry, these authors emphasize a genuinely Christian value in earthly realities and human culture. Since material reality is part of God's creation and has been sanctified in the incarnation, it cannot be destined totally for destruction. Hence, incarnationalists emphasize some point of continuity between history and the kingdom. The resurrection of Christ is the basis for the hope that what is done by human beings in history does in fact contribute to the coming of the kingdom of God.

This viewpoint stands in contrast with that of the eschatologists, among whom we include Louis Bouyer and Jean Daniélou. Shifting the emphasis from the incarnation to the kingdom of God, eschatologists have emphasized the otherness of the kingdom as a pure gift of God's grace which cannot be formed, even partially, by human activity. Since the cross stands between the life of Jesus and the resurrection, these authors emphasize the discontinuity between history and the kingdom. Since we have here "no lasting city" (Heb 13:14), Christians are summoned to be aware of the transitory character of all that transpires in history and of the triviality of all earthly concerns. In language reminiscent of Platonic philosophy, earthly realities are called shadows of the perfect things to come; they are to be discarded with the arrival of the kingdom.

In the tension between these two views we can see the question raised for Christians by Karl Marx in the nineteenth century and again by Ernst Bloch in the twentieth. Does the very nature of Christian eschatological faith alienate human beings from any significant role in human history? Bloch had argued that the call to an eschatological future should turn us to the world with a passionate concern for that future. Instead, Christians have allowed it to turn their attention to "another" world and away from this one.

This problem was one of the concerns of the Christian-Marxist dialogues of the 1960's. That context sheds light on the work of both

Moltmann and Pannenberg. We have spoken in the first chapter of Moltmann's negative dialectic between present and future. To what degree this can be seen as an adequate representation of biblical eschatology remains an open question. However that problem may eventually be solved, it remains true that such a dialectic fails to invest any present moment with significance other than as an instrument of the future. Ratzinger suggests that such a dialectic not only threatens to falsify the Gospel by turning it into a political ideology, but tends to falsify political reality as well. If the future can be won only by the total destruction of the present, and if the mystery of the kingdom can become the basis for irrationality in the political sphere, this seems but another way of saying that grace destroys nature. If so, does this amount to a destruction of human responsibility? (*Esch.*, pp. 19–20). While Moltmann intends to overcome the divorce between faith and worldly involvement, it is far from clear that he has succeeded. Indeed, his form of dialectic appears as a new version of the classical grace-works controversy now formulated in language about the future.

Pannenberg tends to give more emphasis to elements of continuity and transformation than Moltmann allows for. "The Church is true to its vocation only as it anticipates and represents the destiny of all mankind, the goal of history. Whatever significance the Church has for the world depends upon the degree of the Church's devotion to this universal and humanizing vocation."[1]

In the quest for meaning, human existence reveals a "proleptic" structure, i.e. it attempts to "anticipate" the end. It might be better to say—because of the reversal of causality—that human existence is "stamped" by the future to which it is drawn. Therefore, Pannenberg can see positive signs of the kingdom already in the present as the future makes its power felt in history. "Creative love, unloosed by faith and hope, has the power to pierce this fragile and mortal life with flashes of eternal meaning and joy. Thus we can know the peace of wholeness and integrity."[2]

Rahner, in commenting on the *Pastoral Constitution on the Church in the Modern World* (nn. 33–39), points out that the Second Vatican Council summons Christians to work with others in the effort to make the world a more humane place in which to live.[3] This task flows from the very nature of Christian faith. Christians should "allow their eschatological faith to leave its imprint on the structures of earthly life." Paragraph 39 of the Council's text states: "While we are warned that it profits a man nothing if he gain the whole world and lose himself, the expectation of a new earth must not weaken but rather stimulate our concern for cultivating this one. For here grows the body of a new human family, a body which even now is able to give some kind of foreshadowing of the new age." Thus, the Council places the human concern for the future of the world in the context of eschatological hope for a "new heaven and a new earth."

Rahner finds two series of statements juxtaposed by the Council with no clear indication as to how these statements belong together. On the one hand, the Council states that there is a growing human family begun by Christ, that the earthly service to humanity provides "the material of the kingdom of God," that the "new heaven and the new earth" are realized in the transformation of this world and not in its replacement, that it is not only love that remains but also the works produced by love, and that we will find the results of human activity again in the new world. On the other hand, as the Council clearly teaches, the otherworldly vocation of humanity must be distinguished from any merely human task, and the growth of the kingdom of God is not to be identified with earthly progress.

These two types of statements point to the central issue which Rahner highlights in the following: "Is the world which man himself fashions only the 'material' in which he has morally to prove himself, and which in itself remains indifferent? And when the final consummation of the kingdom of God comes, will the world simply be done away with? . . . Or does this second world itself pass, albeit inconceivably 'transformed,' into the *eschaton* properly so called?" (*op. cit.*, p. 266). How seriously do Christians take the world—not only the world of God's creation, but also the world made over by human activity? Does Christian eschatology ultimately weaken the believer's resolve to "build the world"?

Here as elsewhere, Rahner holds the necessity of a dialectical understanding of eschatological statements. On the one hand, the kingdom of God is not merely an abiding stimulus that functions only as a means of keeping history in motion. Rather, it is truly an "act of God" that will "come" and will end history. On the other hand, the coming of the Kingdom can be seen as the self-transcendence of history. The act of God does not have to mean the destruction of human history. It can mean that human history ultimately opens to a future which is fully a future given by God and, at the same time, a future in which human history is preserved and decisively completed.

The nuances of Rahner's dialectical understanding are clearly expressed in his understanding of "categorical future" and "absolute future." By "categorical future" Rahner refers to those futures which human beings can envision, plan for, and bring about in space and time. A "categorical future" is an inner-worldly future made out of worldly elements through human initiative. By "absolute future," on the other hand, Rahner means a total, all-embracing and therefore transcendental fulfillment of the world as a whole. The absolute future, for Rahner, is given by God himself.

While categorical and absolute future may not be identified, they are not unrelated. While categorical futures are the object of human planning and work, the future yet remains open and dark. Each stage accomplished opens new questions. The future is incalculable even at the empirical level. Because of this darkness and openness which seem never to be overcome, Rahner sees in all inner-worldly planning a sign or pointer to an uncontrollable, absolute future. In this way, the absolute future is co-intended as the ultimate goal of all inner-worldly future-planning. The absolute future holds history open and never allows any historical condition, program, or plan to be absolutized. Hope in the absolute future demands concrete, inner-worldly programs and plans, but simultaneously criticizes all such futures lest they be absolutized. This relation between the categorical and the absolute future is basic in Rahner's thought for preserving the value and untouchable meaning of the individual human person. If there were only the categorical future, then the meaning of each present is found only in what it can contribute to a better future on earth. The future becomes a Moloch to which each generation is sacrificed. But if the meaning of the categorical future is relativized by the absolute future, then even the person who can no longer make any concrete contribution to the accomplishment of the inner-worldly future still retains his or her dignity in the light of the absolute future.

Rahner's ideas have influenced the presentation of Schmaus who distinguishes an immanent-transcendent eschatology from one that is purely immanent. While the kingdom of God cannot be identified with

any earthly kingdom, this does not mean that there is no relation whatever. While the Christian future is "not reducible simply to a specific
social, economic, political order in history," Schmaus envisions a
"transformation of the world in the sense of a progressive humanization
of it" (*Dogma* 6, p. 151). Even though secular hopes are but preliminary
with respect to our ultimate goal, still Christians must be concerned
with secular affairs since such activities are the enactment of God's in-
junction to "rule the earth" (Gn 1:28ff). But, as with Rahner, the absolute future relativizes all other futures; they are important but not final
(*op. cit.,* p. 153).

The relation between eschatology and human activity is a basic
concern of theologians of Latin America where it takes the form of a
variety of theologies of praxis (political theology, liberation theology).
Moltmann's theology of hope and Metz's political theology have been
influential here. Both of these European authors had reacted against the
privatizing tendency of existential theology and attempted to develop
critical reflections on the social and political implications of faith. For
both, the effect of the eschatological proclamation of the kingdom and
Jesus' suffering for the sake of the kingdom is a disturbing word, a
"dangerous remembrance."[4] One cannot hear it and remain satisfied
with the status quo.

Echoing these concerns, Latin American theologians such as
Segundo, Boff, and Gutiérrez emphasize that the full meaning of a
faith-confession is to be found in the effect it has in the life of the believer. Their thought reflects a shift from "ortho-doxy" to "ortho-
praxis." The actual concrete life of the believer becomes a criterion for
the truth of what he or she claims to believe. Christianity is not simply
correct ideas, but a renewal of existence which begins to take shape in
historical forms that find fulfillment in the kingdom. The eschatological
faith of Christians must be a transcendent faith not only in theory but in
life-style as well.

From this basic orientation, Latin American liberation theology
emphasizes the social and political dimension of faith and the critical
role of the Church in relation to the social order. It emphasizes strongly
the Christian obligation to become actively engaged in building a better
world, a world marked by greater justice, humanity, and love. The
"coming of the kingdom" is so intimately related to social change that it
is very difficult to distinguish them.

The End of History

Because of the eschatological nature of Christian faith, history has been a problem for Christians from the outset. While the Hebrew Scriptures had looked to an eschatological event in the future, Christians claim that the eschatological event has been realized in the life, death, and resurrection of Jesus. But if the Christian claim is correct, why is it that history continues with no obvious difference in the face of this eschatological event? And if we can see the eschatological event as the goal of history, will history somehow come to an end? For Christian faith, history is bounded by a mystery of absolute origin (= creation) and an absolute future (= eschatology). Does that ultimate limit mean that there must be a temporal limit as well? Will the history of the world come to an end?

It has become common to distinguish the biblical view of history from that of classical antiquity. The later view is symbolized with the circle and has been designated as the "myth of the eternal return" (M. Eliade). This circular understanding of time may be seen as an expression of what Werner Jaeger calls the fatalism which pervaded the religion, philosophy, and literature of antiquity (*Paideia,* Vol. 1). Life is experienced as moving always through the inevitable cycle of life and death. Things undergo change, but within a very limited framework. The most perfect motion is circular—as in the motion of the heavenly bodies—since a circle always returns to its point of origin. "There is nothing new under the sun" says the Book of Ecclesiastes (1:9), a book which reflects the influence of Hellenistic thought patterns.

The biblical experience of time, as reflected in the Pentateuch and the prophetic literature, seems to be quite different and is commonly thought of as a linear experience. It is symbolized with a horizontal line that has both a starting point and a definite end. Particularly in the tradition of Jewish apocalyptic, the whole of created reality is drawn up into historical process moving from creation to consummation. In the apocalyptic event that will end this age, God will vindicate his own act of creation. This history cannot be reduced to anthropology since God is Creator not only of the human race but of the entire cosmos as well. Thus Jewish apocalyptic includes a theology of history which embraces not only the national history of the Jewish people but the history of humanity and of the cosmos. In short, Jewish eschatology and apocalyptic pushes into reflection on universal history.

This tradition provided significant factors for the context within which Jesus preached the coming of God's kingdom. Likewise it was crucial for the emergence of Christian faith in the resurrection of Christ. Thus from its very beginning, Christian faith has raised the question of universal history and of the goal toward which all history is directed. Christian theology that intends to deal seriously with these historical beginnings must deal with a real future, that is, with a future which is not yet a reality and which will not be realized independently of a temporal, historical process. One cannot talk of the goal to which all history is directed without creating the expectation that somehow, somewhere, the course of history will come to an end.

It is possible to use the term "end" in a variety of ways. The usage that comes to mind most readily takes "end" in a strictly temporal sense. To speak of the end of history in this sense is to speak of the last chronological moment after which there will be no history. But another usage can be distinguished. "End" can refer to a goal, or to a finality of purpose. Here, to speak of the end of history is to speak of the purpose which God has in creating the world and the human race with its history. As John A.T. Robinson writes, "though there is no necessity that finality of purpose should automatically be marked by temporal cessation, such is the inevitable form of expression by which this finality is asserted."[5]

1. *Annihilation.* Though it seems almost inevitable that the finality of history will be expressed in temporal terms, the distinction between these two meanings of "end" provides the basis for a variety of viewpoints among theologians. In fundamentalist circles and in popular literature, the end of history is commonly pictured as the moment of the great conflagration. When history has run its course, the world will be annihilated by fire. This seems to be the clear meaning of texts such as 2 Peter 3:7–13. Yet, in 1459, Pope Pius II condemned an opinion which held that "the world must naturally be consumed and end, the heat of the sun consuming the humidity of the earth and of the air, so that the elements are set on fire" (DS 717). And Aquinas in the thirteenth century held that nothing would ever be annihilated (*S. Th.* I, q. 104, a. 4). These traditional views should serve as a caution for those who are inclined to read the text of 2 Peter as a literal description of a cosmic

event. In 1950, exegete Ernest Lussier argued that Scripture is silent about the future of the physical world. From an exegetical perspective, the fire of the last day is better seen as a symbol of the irresistible power of divine judgment and justice than as a description of the destruction of the physical universe.[6]

Scripture seems to be far more concerned with the day of the Lord or with the parousia of Christ than it is with the destiny of the physical world. A. Winklhofer writes that the return of Christ brings with it "the last day of history and of the world in its present form."[7] But we cannot claim that the return of Christ "will coincide with a natural end of the world."[8] We await not annihilation but a "new heaven and a new earth."

2. *An End for History.* In an extended exegetical study,[9] Anton Vögtle argues that the Christian Scriptures offer no adequate basis for any predictions about the end of history; these texts teach nothing about the future of the cosmos. From a systematic perspective G. Greshake comes to a similar conclusion. Matter itself cannot be brought to perfection. It is perfectible only in relation to humanity. If we view perfection as an endless, dynamic process of transition from "this aeon to that aeon," then there is no need to postulate an end.[10] This position which holds that there is nothing in Christian faith that necessarily implies an end of history in a temporal sense stands in striking contrast to the views of Pannenberg, Ratzinger, and Rahner.

Pannenberg's theology as a whole is cast within the framework of "universal history." Revelation, and indeed all of reality, unfolds in a history. But history receives its perfection and its unity from the goal toward which it is moving in time.[11] Jesus' preaching of the kingdom of God implies that the unity of the world is to be expected from its future. The futurity with which Pannenberg is concerned involves not only existential time but chronological time as well. To speak of universal history in such a context must imply that our present mode of experience of spatial-temporal realities will be transcended. In this sense at least, history will end.

Rahner is explicit in his criticism of purely existential eschatology. He refers to it as a form of Platonizing theology which cannot adequately cope with the concrete, material world. Christian salvation is not an escape from the world which leaves materiality behind. Rather, it is the salvation of the world. Christian theology, argues Rahner, must speak of a real future not simply in terms of existential time, but in terms of a real passage through chronological time from past to present to future. The final state of the world does not really exist as yet; "it will come at a certain point but has not come as yet" (*Inv.* 4, pp. 352–53).

Thus Rahner can write quite explicitly: "This world in its totality has a beginning and a history; it goes on toward a point which is not the end of its existence but the end of its unfinished and continually self-propagating history" (*op. cit.,* pp. 351–52). History, as Rahner conceives it, is the unfinished movement toward perfection. When perfection is realized, the movement toward it is finished and history is brought to an end, both temporally and in terms of finality. "We know . . . from the testimony of God that this history of the world will come to an end, and that this end will not be a sheer cessation, a 'being-no-longer' of the world itself, but the participation in the perfection of the spirit" (*op. cit.,* pp. 352–53).

Ratzinger argues in a similar way. The Christian faith implies the rejection of any claim that the world can be brought to perfection within history and from resources purely immanent to it. This negative statement is counterpointed by a positive one. The world will be brought to its end by the indestructibility of that divine love which has been victorious in Christ. History is fulfilled only by transcending itself. "The risen Christ is the living certainty that this transcendence—without which the world is absurd—does not open into emptiness, and that, therefore, history can be lived positively, and that our poor, limited, rational efforts are meaningful. From this perspective, the anti-Christ is the unconditional closing off of history to its own logic" (*Esch.,* p. 175). If there is not an end to history, argues Ratzinger, the fundamental meaning of history will remain undecided (*Esch.,* p. 156; *Introd.,* p. 245).

All these views may be seen as attempts to give a coherent account—by whatever philosophical aids—to two dimensions of the Christian resurrection-faith and of the apocalyptic tradition which was of crucial importance in the emergence of Christian faith. Jewish apocalyptic had believed that the whole of history will find a unified meaning in the future act of God that would bring this age to an end and inaugurate the final, eschatological age. Christian resurrection-faith has traditionally claimed that precisely this has happened in the resurrection of Jesus Christ. Secondly, the apocalyptic tradition had believed that God would vindicate his own act of creation; he would bring the world to fulfillment. Therefore, salvation is the salvation of God's creation. The early Christian faith had maintained these concrete expectations. Through the resurrection, the created world—in Jesus—has found its fulfilling goal in union with God. Serious Christian reflection cannot responsibly ignore these claims. No such thing as a unified meaning for the whole of history is conceivable except from that point at which one can see the whole—that is, from the end. But the question of the end is not adequately dealt with unless one deals with the materiality and temporality of God's created world.

The great biblical metaphors of the end need not be seen as descriptions of the physical end of the cosmos. But they can serve to alert us to the mystery of our future. And they can stimulate reflection on the mystery of the world which we believe to be the fruit of God's creative goodness and the object of his redemptive love. The theological concept of the end calls for a transformation of our categories of space, time, and matter.

5
Parousia: The Central Metaphor

The Parousia of Christ

The central Christian metaphor for the end of history is the parousia or the second coming of Christ. Around this center is a cluster of related themes: judgment, resurrection of the dead, heaven and hell, the kingdom, the new heaven and the new earth. It is the "coming of the Lord" that "brings history to its fulfillment."[1]

Parousia is a Greek word which means presence or arrival. It is used to designate the presence of the coming of Christ. In Scripture the time of the parousia is indefinite. Matthew writes that the disciples will not have finished making the rounds of the cities of Israel before the Son of Man comes (Mt 10:23). But both Matthew (24:36) and Mark (13:32) insist that the hour is known to no one, not even to the Son of Man. It is known only to the Father. At times the Scriptures emphasize the need to be ready because the Son of Man will come with no previous announcement like a thief in the night. Elsewhere the Synoptic Gospels describe the signs of his coming which, though obscure, should yet be clear enough to alert the watchful. It is clear that the images used to speak of the parousia are derived from the description of the coming of the Son of Man in the apocalyptic tradition (Dn 7:13ff). According to this tradition, the coming of the Son of Man will be the final event of history. With it will come the establishment of the kingdom of God and the victory of God over all powers hostile to his will. It is not difficult to see the parallel between this Jewish tradition and the Christian description of the parousia of Christ.

John McKenzie states that the apocalyptic imagery involved here should be taken precisely as imagery. Therefore he warns that these images should lead Christians "to draw no unwarranted conclusions in detail about the external features of the parousia."[2]

The complexity of the Scriptures calls for great care in drawing out any theological implications from the material pertaining to the parousia of Christ. In an influential study on the resurrection,[3] F.X. Durwell wrote of the parousia in lines that reflect the etymology of the Greek word. The parousia is not a return at the end of history of a Christ who has been absent from the world since Good Friday. Rather, it signals the full working out of what was begun in the resurrection. "From the moment of his glorification, Christ's parousia has been in the world. . . . Christ's resurrection and the manifestation of his glory, together with his final coming, form a single mystery of the parousia, revealed gradually in the course of history. . . . For us on earth it (= time) shows one by one the effects of the parousia of Christ which will eventually be revealed as a whole" (*Resurrection*, pp. 254–56).

This statement reflects themes that have become common in theological treatments of the parousia. Already in the 1940's, Romano Guardini wrote of the return of Christ from the perspective of judgment. "The doctrine of the Last Judgment is, at bottom, a revelation of Christ. . . . It implies seeing Christ in everything, carrying His image in our hearts with such intensity that it lifts us above the world, above history and the works of man, and enables us to see those things for what they are, to weigh them and assign to them their eternal value, in a word, to be their judges."[4]

For Rahner, the parousia is the final stage of the one, unified coming of God to the world in a history that finds its center in the person of Christ. From a Christological perspective, the parousia is the universal manifestation of Christ's Lordship. From the perspective of creation-theology, the parousia is the arrival of the world at its destiny. This view unites a number of themes characteristic of German theology that has been influenced by nineteenth century philosophical idealism. The concept of a universal history in which God enters into revelatory self-communication with the world draws much of its inspiration from this source. This view of history is given a Christian interpretation by seeing the coming together of God and humanity in Christ as the center and goal of the entire movement of history. The parousia is not the return of a Lord who has been absent, but the breaking through of a presence that has been continuous throughout history.

This is expressed succinctly in the description of the parousia as "the permanent blessed presence of Christ in the manifest finality of the history of the world and of salvation which is perfected and ended in the destiny of Jesus Christ" (*Encyc.*, pp. 1158–60). All other statements about the Last Things reflect partial aspects of this one, fundamental mystery: God at one with the world in Christ. Since this represents the definitive state of the world and of humanity, it includes the destiny of each as an individual person before God and as a member of the human race in its entirety. Thus it includes statements of the personal aspects of death, particular judgment, beatific vision, or hell. But it includes as well statements about the general aspects of parousia such as the resurrection of the dead, the general judgment, the kingdom of God, and the cosmic fulfillment of God's creative activity (*op. cit.*, p. 821).

Because the parousia is ultimately a free and incalculable act of God, Rahner holds that we cannot know the time at which this act of God will bring history to an end; for it is known to God alone, and God has not revealed it (Mk 13:32). Since the parousia involves the fulfillment of the world and of humanity in all its dimensions, it will have a "concrete form of being, though one which at present escapes our understanding" (*op. cit.*, pp. 1158–60).

Schmaus presents a similar view (*Dogma* 6, pp. 177–79). The return of Christ is not a spatial event but a personal experience. The resurrected mode of Christ's existence will have been so thoroughly actualized in the world that it can no longer be veiled. The whole of the world and history will be penetrated and transformed by the power of the resurrection. The scriptural image of the Son of Man appearing in the heavens is to be taken as a figurative expression. Similarly, the sound of mighty trumpets is a symbolic means of evoking the awareness that the power of the glorified Lord will be irresistible when it is made manifest to all.

Ratzinger agrees that it is possible to evoke an awareness of the parousia only by means of images. We can get no information about future cosmic events from the biblical images. Much of this imagery belongs to the language of an ancient liturgical tradition. The parousia is the highest realization of that which takes place already in the eucharistic liturgy: the meeting of God and the world. Christian liturgy is the ritual enactment of a life lived in the power of the risen Lord. Thus, liturgy, life, and resurrection are brought together most intimately. The living out of Christ's command of love in the power of the Spirit is the heart of Christian life. It is likewise that which lies at the core of Christian liturgy. So, Ratzinger can write: "In that love which enacts his commands, his coming takes place in the midst of the world as an eschatological event" (*Esch.*, p. 167). The full realization of the parousia is the final realization of the Easter-mystery. Meanwhile, in every approach to the risen Lord, the Church approaches the parousia. In its worship and in its actions, it prays and lives into the parousia. Hence, Ratzinger concludes, the parousia is not speculation about the unknown future but is a clarification of Christian life and liturgy (*op. cit.*, p. 168). Faith in the return of Christ means, for Ratzinger, that the believer rejects the idea that the world can bring itself to perfection from its own resources within history. Human hope is not limited to the laboratories of science but is directed ultimately to that truth and love that transcends history and has been victorious in Christ.

Robinson emphasizes the Christological meaning of the return of Christ. It is a fundamental Christian claim that God's purpose has been realized in the personal history and destiny of Jesus. However strongly one may affirm this, such a claim stands in dialectical tension with the fact that God's purpose has not yet been realized in the fullest sense. Evidence of this is found in the fact that the external flow of history continues as before, and our experience seems to show clearly that God's will is not yet all in all (*In the End*, p. 70). The second coming is necessary, according to Robinson, as a statement about the eschatological significance of the processes of life and death, salvation and judgment set in motion by the incarnation. The parousia cannot be pictured literally as a future event, for "it is 'the revelation of our Lord Jesus Christ,' the lightning-flash which lays bare to public gaze the naked truth about the world and the situation of every man in it, as at any given moment the individual stands on one side of the line or the other, for Christ or against him" (*op. cit.*, p. 80). Parousia universalizes and clarifies "what must happen, and is already happening, whenever the Christ comes in love and comes in power, wherever are to be traced the signs of his presence and the marks of his cross" (*ibid.*). Parousia symbolizes the eschatological dimensions of every day. Yet that is not all.

Parousia not only transects the historical process, but it consummates history as well. The whole of history has a meaning and goal. This also is expressed in Christian terms by the parousia of Christ.

Such approaches to the metaphor of the parousia make it clear why many theologians hold that—while the Christian faith believes the world has a future—faith offers no explicit knowledge of the final state of our planet just as it offers no specific knowledge of its first state. To think that the Bible offers us such information if we could only interpret it correctly is a serious and potentially dangerous illusion.

Signs of the End

The Synoptic Gospels give vivid images of cosmic signs that will precede the parousia (Mt 24:29; Mk 13:24; Lk 21:25–27). How are these images to be understood in relation to statements that describe the coming of the Son of Man like a thief in the night, and to Christ's statement that the Father alone knows the time of his coming?

Ratzinger summarizes the pertinent exegetical materials by distinguishing two strands of scriptural tradition (*Esch.*, pp. 160–65). The first strand sees no possibility of reckoning the time of Christ's coming while the second tradition speaks of signs. This strange duality in the Scriptures reflects two dimensions of the mystery of Christ. The Church confesses the divinity and the humanity of Jesus. In confessing his divinity, we confess the immediacy of God's presence in Jesus. On the other hand, in confessing his humanity, we confess that Christ acts as a human being through historical mediation. This means that the coming of God in Christ is purely an act of God, but that this act of God is inseparably tied to history. Ratzinger argues that Christ is both the "incalculable, inner completion as well as the chronological end" of time.

This Christological reflection sheds light on the duality of the scriptural statements concerning the second coming. Insofar as Christ is purely an act of God, there is no possibility of reckoning his coming in temporal categories. Since he is the Other who comes from beyond, his coming cannot be dated. The only answer to questions about signs and warnings is: "What I say to you, I say to all: Be on guard" (Mk 13:37). But the same chapter of Mark's Gospel speaks of signs. This is seen by Ratzinger to reflect the other side of the Christological confession, namely, that God acts through historical mediation. The coming of God to the world is not unrelated to the experience of temporality in the world.

More than other authors, Ratzinger offers reflections specifically on the signs mentioned in Mark 13. There we read of the widespread growth of evil, of wars and catastrophes, of persecution and of powers that might be called the anti-Christ. From this, two conclusions may be drawn. First, the signs seem to say that what precedes the end is not an age of historical maturity but the inner collapse of history. Second, a close look at world history shows that these signs may well be characteristics of all historical periods. Even the anti-Christ is a principle of Church history experienced by each age in its own way. Ratzinger concludes that the signs do not make it possible to date the end of history. Rather, they describe the coming of Christ in history in such a way that "every age is in need of vigilance" (*Esch.*, p. 164). The signs indicate that the world always touches on the totally Other who will at some point end all chronological time.

Schmaus interprets Mark 13 and Luke 17 in a similar way. The question about the time of the end must remain an open question since Christ himself refused to give an answer to it (Mk 13:22; Mt 24:36–44; 25:1–40). The parousia material is very likely based on the teaching of Jesus, but in its present form it is reworked in the light of the community's experience for use in Christian catechesis. As it now stands, it is an exhortation to watchfulness with a strong eschatological orientation (*Dogma* 6, p. 184).

Robinson draws an explicit parallel between the account of the fall in Genesis and the scriptural texts which speak of the end. A similar dynamic is operative in the composition of these texts concerning the beginning and end. Both flow from the present experience of the author. The writer of Genesis is interested not in people who lived thousands of years ago but with people of his own age and of every age. In trying to account for the pervasiveness of evil in a world created by a loving God, the author creates a story that expresses in concrete images many dimensions of human responsibility for the condition of the world. Thus the present experience of good and evil is made to flow into the past until it is anchored at the beginning. The account of the beginning is shaped by the present of the author. Similarly in the texts pertaining to the end, the point of departure is the present. All the elements in these texts are "first and foremost descriptions of *present* realities within the life of the New Age" (*In the End*, p. 77).

As a specific application of this view, Robinson argues that the "coming" of Christ happens in the sending of the Spirit, that the resurrection of the body occurs when one puts on the new person in the body of Christ, that the anti-Christ is present wherever one gives a final refusal to the Gospel, and that the Last Judgment is being wrought in every moment of choice and decision (*ibid.*). While each of these is a present reality, none can be understood simply in terms of the present. As in Genesis the present flows into reflection on the past, so here the present flows into reflection on the future. When this happens, the resurrection of the body, the anti-Christ, and the judgment are associated with the last day. The cluster of symbols whereby Christians evoke an awareness of the eschatological significance of history as a whole thus emerges out of the present experience of faith and grace.

Resurrection of the Dead

However one understands the destiny of the individual immediately upon death, the notion of an interim condition arises at the point where we consciously relate the individual to the collective future of the human race. No individual is "complete" until the whole is "complete." One of the basic symbols used by Christians to express the end of the interim condition and the realization of the collective destiny of humanity is that of the general resurrection. The idea of a general or collective resurrection is intimately related to the early Christian understanding of the resurrection of Christ. Insofar as the resurrection of Christ is understood from the context of apocalyptic, it represents in the person of Jesus the anticipation of the collective future of the redeemed. While the doctrine of the resurrection at the end of history has been maintained over the centuries by Eastern and Western Christianity, and in the West by both Protestants and Catholics, it has been rejected just as consistently by Gnostics, Manicheans, and a variety of rationalists down to the present time.

Summarizing some of John Baillie's reflections on human destiny,[5] Robinson distinguishes doctrines of survival, of immortality, and of resurrection (*In the End,* pp. 85ff). This distinction helps to focus on the peculiar nature of Christian hope. Each of these models is a way of attempting to give an account of what happens when a human person dies. Survival theories hold that we simply go on to another life which is not essentially different from this. Such an existence is thought at times to be at least somewhat pleasurable. At other times it is thought to be unpleasant, or, at best, neutral. By way of contrast, theories of immortality are convinced that there is a divine spark in the human person. This is commonly identified with the highest or the deepest dimension of the human soul which is thought to be a part of the divine spirit. Imprisoned in the body during history, the soul will return at death to be reunited with the divine. Such theories never arrive at a personal immortality, nor do they find it possible to deal with the body in a positive way.

Against these two types of theories, the Christian hope stands out with its own characteristics. Christian hope looks not to survival nor to salvation of a spiritual part of human nature, nor to the absorption of individuality into a formless absolute. On the contrary, it looks to the transforming fulfillment of humanity in all its dimensions: individual and social, spiritual and corporal. Its hope rests not on something in humanity being naturally immortal but on the life-giving, creative love of God. Therefore, Christianity's doctrine of resurrection must speak of the individual resurrection and of the collective resurrection. It must speak not only of the soul but also of the body and of material reality.

Robinson discusses the resurrection of the body against the background of some insights of biblical anthropology. There, so writes Robinson, the body is that by which a person is inserted into a rich and constantly shifting network of relations to other persons and the world. Understood in such a context, the resurrection of the body is a statement about human solidarity. "It is an assertion that no individual can be saved apart from the whole" (*op. cit.*, p. 100). The Christian hope is not that the individual will be saved by escaping from this mass of relationships or by escaping from history and nature. On the contrary, Christianity hopes for the salvation of humanity in and with the world and its history. It looks to "the redeeming of all the myriad relationships of creation into a new heaven and a new earth, the city of God, the body of Christ" (*ibid.*). The body—in biblical anthropology—represents not individuality but solidarity. Therefore the denial of the body's redemption and restoration immediately after death "stands for the great truth that no one can fully be saved apart from his brother, or indeed apart from the whole of creation. It is only in the last day when all things are restored that the new corporality will be complete" (*op. cit.*, p. 109).

Questions concerning the resurrection of the dead in contemporary theology are obscured by new forms of anthropology as well as by new approaches to the theology of death. Many modern anthropologies have difficulty with the idea of a soul existing after death independently of a body. They prefer to emphasize the basic unity of the human person in a way that makes such a notion almost inconceivable. Similarly, theological reflections on death and on the destiny of the individual person have led some to argue that the resurrection of the individual follows immediately on the person's death.

Such views can be developed into quite distinct eschatological viewpoints. Some authors envision an immediate resurrection at death but see this as a provisional condition that does not deny a general resurrection at the end of history. Others see this immediate resurrection to make both an interim condition and a general resurrection superfluous.

This latter view of a resurrection in death is strongly espoused by Gisbert Greshake, Gerhard Lohfink, Ladislaus Boros, and Wilhelm Breuning.[6] Without approving any specific form of this theory, Rahner holds it as a possible opinion that the "single and total perfecting of man in 'body' and 'soul' takes place immediately after death, that the resurrection of the flesh and the general judgment take place 'parallel' to the temporal history of the world" (*Inv.* 17, p. 115). Lohfink has tried to clarify and justify the theory of resurrection in death by employing an understanding of time reminiscent of Karl Barth. The coming of God is equally distant and equally near to every point of earthly time. The fulfillment of history—which Lohfink sees as a basic biblical concern—takes place not at some hypothetical end-point of cosmic time, but at every point of time in human history. There is no reason why the coming of God should be associated with the death of those living in the last human generation. Rather, according to Lohfink, the coming of God coincides with the death of each and every human person regardless of when they have lived in history (*Naherwartung,* pp. 61–62). According to this view, the individual person in death experiences not only his or her personal eschaton, but, together with it, the eschaton of the entire history of the world which is simultaneous with the individual and comes to an end with the individual.

This sort of theory has sparked debate. It would not be true to say that the authors who espouse various forms of this theory focus on the individual to the detriment of the collective dimension of eschatology.

Greshake and Lohfink, in dependence on Greshake, deal with the collective impressively by making use of relational categories. While the theory is helpful in gaining some insight on past history, its principal weakness lies in its unconvincing implications for our understanding of future history. If human history is truly a history of freedom, the future remains open and undetermined. What remains as a potential and undetermined future cannot really "be with" the individual who dies before that potential has been determined and made actual.

Ratzinger has criticized the theory of Greshake and Lohfink for failing to take account of the materiality of the resurrection. Drawing from insights of Aquinas, Rahner, and Teilhard, Ratzinger argues firmly against all attempts to reject materiality from the ultimate fulfillment of created reality. The object of God's creative and salvific will is the world. And the world is a world of material and spiritual reality. To exclude either of these from the fulfillment which constitutes salvation is arbitrary. Serious theology must discuss both.

One need only think of the mysteries of modern physics to sense how little we know about the nature of material reality even in its present form, to say nothing of some future form. Ratzinger clearly recognizes the difficulty of any attempt to conceptualize what the new form of material existence might be like. One cannot adequately conceptualize the new world. Nor can one make any concrete statements about the nature of humanity's relation to materiality in the new world.

But, argues Ratzinger, we are certain that the dynamism of the cosmos is oriented to a goal. From a biblical perspective, the goal of creation is the fulfillment of all dimensions of created reality, not the fulfillment of only a part. Therefore, materiality cannot be excluded from a theological understanding of fulfillment. From a more philosophical perspective, history may be seen as a movement toward unity. Therefore, a final situation in which matter and spirit would simply stand in juxtaposition to each other with no real relation would contradict the essential meaning of history (*Esch.*, p. 159; *Introd.*, p. 277). What Ratzinger sees as the final state of the world is a situation in which matter and spirit will be related to each other in a new and definitive way. This hope for the future of the world remains the concrete content of the Church's confession of the resurrection of the flesh (*Esch.*, p. 160). In view of the pervasiveness of materialistic ideologies and the modern cult of the body, Ratzinger sees a particular significance in a religious vision that, by its very nature, must deal with the destiny of material reality in some way.

Similarly, Rahner sees history in terms of a dialectical relation between spirit and matter. History is, in essence, the unfinished movement toward fulfillment. The future that we hope for is ultimately a *human* future. Therefore, it is the fulfillment of our human being in all its dimensions. Because of our nature as incarnate spirit, our final perfection must include both spirit and corporality. Christ's victory at the end of history will not mean the disappearance of the material world but its transformation. Those who share in Christ's final victory will be not disembodied souls, but fully human members of a perfect society which will live as the "whole Christ" on his glorified earth.[7]

In line with the strong Christological orientation which he has taken over the years, Schmaus suggests that the glorified humanity of the risen Christ is an appropriate point of departure for any systematic understanding of eschatology. The world must be explained in terms of the risen Christ. This conviction Schmaus works out in terms of an evolutionary view of history inspired by Teilhard. From a scriptural perspective, Genesis 2–3 and Romans 8 suggest that the destiny of the world is intimately intertwined with human destiny. Evolution, as Schmaus understands it, is not the work of matter alone. The potential of material reality is brought to actuality through human work and through the ever-present creative action of God. Each stage of evolution includes both a dynamism from below and a dynamism from above. In such a view, materiality can be seen as radically open to the transforming power of God which brings it to ever greater levels of fulfillment. Without becoming specific in details, Schmaus concludes: "The thought is not fantastic that matter might attain a mode of existence similar to that of the glorified Christ and of humanity gathered into unity in him" (*Dogma* 6, p. 213).

The risen Christ is the prototype of humanity's future. Schmaus sees the parousia and the general resurrection as the final revelation of Christ. It is here that Christ calls all of humanity and the whole of creation to himself so as to lead all to the Father. Here is found the fullness of life in its final and perfect form. Everything hurtful to life or contrary to unity is excluded. Since the call of Christ is spoken in the power of God's creative love, it has such compelling force that nothing can resist it (*op. cit.*, p. 187).

The authors treated here work from the conviction that the God who creates is identical with the God who saves and who brings creation to its ultimate fulfillment. Indeed, God creates the world with a view to its final perfection. The path from creation to consummation is the history of interaction between God and humanity. By creating the kind of world he has in fact created, God has freely made himself dependent on the free response of human persons in bringing about his ultimate purpose for the world. Therefore, eschatology is the ultimate extension of the relation between the world and God. The kingdom is neither God alone nor humanity alone, but the fullness of the free, loving relationship that has been brought about through history. God is he "who brings the dead to life and calls into being what does not exist" (Rom 4:17). God creates humanity "from nothing," but he does not recreate it "from nothing." God does not annihilate his first creation in order to begin again from nothing. The "new creation" of which eschatology speaks is here seen as the transforming completion of the fruit of God's first creative act. In the resurrection, God vindicates his own act of creation. He does not create another world from nothing, but brings this present world to its final perfection. It is this concern that lies behind the emphasis which these authors give to some level of continuity between present and future, between creation and consummation, between history and eschatology.

6
The Possibility of Eternal Damnation

Judgment and Purgation

It is a common religious conviction that human beings are responsible for their actions and must eventually render an account before God. The Christian Scriptures connect judgment with the return of Christ. This reflects the conviction that human decisions and actions are important and must be seen in terms of the person's relation to Christ.

God is the ultimate source of judgment on the unrighteousness of the world. But, Ratzinger argues, God has turned over judgment "to one who, as man, is our brother. It is not a stranger who judges us but he whom we know in faith. The judge will not advance to meet us as the quite other, but as one of us, who knows human existence from inside and has suffered" (*Introd.*, p. 251). This Christological orientation is developed further in Ratzinger's *Eschatologie* to make explicit mention of the Church (*Esch.*, p. 168). Here Ratzinger points out that in the Scriptures judgment is rendered by God, by Christ, by the Twelve, and by the saints. The basis of judgment is simply the truth that is God. But this truth has given itself to be known in Christ in the form of love. Here Ratzinger sees the connection between God and Christ in terms of judgment. Humanity will be judged in relation to the divine truth which has revealed itself as self-giving love in Jesus' life. What then of the Twelve and the saints? These express the fact that Christ does not stand alone but always together with his body which constitutes his fullness. Our encounter with Christ includes our encounter with the brothers and sisters of Christ. Thus, the Church, or the communion of saints, also enters into judgment.

Similarly for Schmaus, judgment means that a human person gives himself or herself over to the "measure of all things and accepts the measure of God as it appears in Jesus Christ—that is, the love, holiness, and justice of God realized in Jesus" (*Dogma* 6, p. 236). From the human side, Schmaus describes the moment of general judgment as "a flash of illumination wherein everyone can see in an instant the whole course of history and the part every individual has played in it. . . . The enlightenment arising out of God's truth is so powerful in its effect that no one can resist it. . . . The norm of judgment is love, that love which appears in Jesus Christ . . ." (*op. cit.,* p. 202).

Related to judgment is the notion of purgation. Here the question arises whether there can be an increase in perfection for the dead, or whether there can be a purification. The Roman Catholic Church affirms such a possibility. Rahner clarifies the Church's teaching by affirming that the perfection of the human person is first of all an act of God's grace. But it is also a process that takes place in time. Whatever suffering may be involved in this process is not extrinsic to the process but comes precisely from the lack of harmony between God's intention and the fundamental option that undergirds a particular human life. One does not make a new fundamental option in death. Rather, the style of life that has preceded death comes to maturity in the final moment of life. However, the finality of human decision in death does not mean that all the dimensions of human reality are integrated into this decision. So, in Rahner's view, the process of integration may be thought of as continuing after death. In view of the possibility of a loving communication of all human beings in Christ, it is possible that this process can be supported by the prayer of others.[1]

Von Balthasar and Ratzinger see a process of transformation similar to that envisioned by Rahner. Through this process, a person is prepared for God and for the communion of saints. These two authors emphasize the personal encounter with Jesus, the Lord, in death. He himself is the "fire of judgment." Ratzinger writes that "purification is effected through nothing other than the transforming power of the Lord who melts our closed heart and burns it free so that it fits well into the living organism of His body" (*Esch.,* p. 187). Purification is not something laid on the human person from outside but is an intrinsic aspect of the transformation necessary for us to become capable of existing in Christ, in God, and in unity with the communion of saints (*op. cit.*, p. 188). Since the transforming element of this encounter with Christ transcends earthly time-measurements, it would be naive to try to determine whether it is short or long in terms of physical measurements (*op. cit.*, p. 187). Earthly measurements of time cannot be applied to the moment of this encounter.

Eternal Damnation

Theological reflection in the last ten years has attempted to go beyond the mere repetition of traditional statements about hell by distinguishing the intended meaning of these statements from the specific images used to communicate that meaning. It has become a common conviction that statements about hell must be read against the background of the total Gospel. Central to the Scriptures is the redemptive death and resurrection of Jesus in which God reveals himself as the merciful Lord of history. From this comes the conviction that statements about heaven and hell are not on the same level. Heaven is a metaphor that elicits an awareness of the *reality* of that definitive salvation accomplished in Christ. Salvation refers to the loving, saving will of God which is directed to all human beings and to the definitive success of the history between God and humanity. Hell, on the other hand, expresses the real *possibility* that a person can close himself or herself to the grace of God and thus may choose isolation instead of communion with God. The image of hell makes us aware of the seriousness of human decisions. Most theologians see the possibility of a definitive rejection of God as intrinsically connected with human freedom. But it remains an open question whether any human person has ever gone that way. Vorgrimler recalls the historical fact that, despite the enormous authority of Augustine, the Roman Catholic Church has not accepted the doctrine of a double predestination. The conviction that some persons have been saved is reflected in the cult of the saints. But there never has been a negative conviction parallel to this concerning the real damnation of any individual.[2]

According to Rahner, it is inappropriate to think of hell as a sort of vindictive punishment such as that demanded by civil society for those who infringe the social order (*Encyc.*, p. 604). Yet, the possibility to which the word "hell" refers must be maintained, for "hell" and the other metaphors such as fire, worms, and darkness all point to the same thing: " . . . the possibility of man being finally lost and estranged from God in all the dimensions of his existence" (*Encyc.*, p. 603).

The possibility of an eternity of hell springs from human obduracy which is grounded in human freedom. "Freedom is the will and the possibility of positing the definitive" (*Encyc.*, p. 604). It is not to be thought of as the possibility of endless revisions of our decisions. And "eternity" is not the endless duration of time after the history of freedom, but is the definitive fruit of history.

Hell, according to Rahner, is not to be thought of as something external to human decisions, added on as an arbitrary punishment. It is the intrinsic effect of human decisions. God is "active" in the punishment of hell only insofar as he does not release the human person from the ultimate results of his or her own action, even though that person's condition is in contradiction to God's intent. Hence, the notion of vindictive punishment is not helpful in shedding light on the doctrine of hell.

For Ratzinger, the idea of eternal damnation has a firm place in the teaching of Jesus (*Esch.*, p. 176). Like Rahner, Ratzinger sees the doctrine of hell as related to human freedom. What is really at stake is the conviction that God maintains an unconditional respect for the freedom of his creatures (*op. cit.*, p. 177). If freedom is the freedom to love, it must inevitably include the freedom to refuse love. Therefore, it would be a mistake to see the doctrine as a sort of "objectifying speculation about the other world."[3] The real intent of the doctrine is to underscore the seriousness of human existence and of human action. Only if we live in the light of the real possibility of eternal failure can we see ourselves with utmost seriousness. "Hell is wanting-only-to-be-oneself; what happens when man barricades himself up in himself" (*Introd.*, p. 239).

L. Boros reflects the same line of thought. "Hell is not something that simply happens from outside; it is not something that God imposes on us afterwards for our misdeeds. . . . It is the mode of existence of a human being who is satisfied in himself, for all eternity; he has nothing more and desires nothing more than himself. . . . There is no tragic grandeur about hell because fundamentally there can not be any 'place' which is hell. There is only a state of heart."[4]

Schmaus points out the danger of trying to localize hell. While the doctrine of hell appears to many as a scandal, it is in fact essential to Christian teaching. The themes which stand out in Schmaus' treatment are love and isolation. Reflecting the same concern for human freedom as found in Rahner and Ratzinger, Schmaus describes the essence of hell as that form of life which a person chooses when the person cuts himself or herself off from the love of God and other human beings in order to be the motive and measure of all personal planning and personal effort. "When sin in all its forms . . . is understood as a failure to love, then hell can be understood as the final fixation in this state" (*Dogma* 6, p. 253). Hell is in essence a revolt against love whereby the person becomes totally self-enclosed and incapable of dialogue with others (*op. cit.,* p. 255). With a strong focus on an anthropological understanding, Schmaus writes: " . . . man carries hell within himself; he is not cast into it, as into an abyss, but himself creates it" (*op. cit.,* p. 254). The endlessness of hell is created not by God but by the human person through the person's decisive choice against love.

Universalism

Rahner, Ratzinger, and Schmaus reflect what is, by far, the more common position among Catholic theologians: namely, the possibility of hell as the eternal separation from God must be retained as a necessary implication of human freedom. While this may be called the "majority report," it is not the only position found among theologians. Since the time of Origen, there have been those who feel that the notion of an eternal hell is repugnant to a God of love, and who hold that eventually all human persons will be saved.

This view, often called "universalism," is clearly rejected by Rahner as "presumptuous" (*Inv.* 4, pp. 338–39). The conflict between universalists and non-universalists reflects different views on the nature of human freedom. John Hick speaks of an impasse in the discussion caused by the fact that, though many would like to hold universalism, it seems impossible to reconcile such an opinion with human freedom (*Death and Eternal Life,* p. 242).

Rahner speaks for the non-universalist position when he says that freedom does not mean that the human person can always revise decisions. On the contrary, "freedom is the will and the possibility of positing the definitive" (*Encyc.*, p. 604). In Rahner's view, death is the moment of final and irrevocable decision, and eternity is the definitive achievement of history. At the moment of death, each person either ratifies or reverses the fundamental choice carried out during life. The result of this decision is either salvation or damnation. God never over- rides human freedom to release people from their freely chosen condi- tion. To affirm the possibility of hell is a necessary implication of Rahner's concept of freedom. But to affirm even the possibility of hell is contradictory to the universalist position as reflected in Robinson and Hick.

Robinson sees the non-universalist position to be caught in an un- fortunate dilemma. One must choose between human freedom or divine coercion. If we are truly free, hell is a possibility. If God's salvific will must necessarily be realized fully, we must reckon with coercion on the part of God. But this dilemma, says Robinson, is not necessary.

His own approach leans heavily on divine mercy which can be ap- plied even to the notion of judgment. Judgment is absolutely necessary, writes Robinson. "But the sole possible function of judgment can be to enable men to receive the mercy which renders it superfluous. . . . Only if and when all men respond with that 'yes' which they are called into being to give, can God utter the final 'consummatum'" (*In the End*, p. 117). According to Robinson, even the possibility that some people may be eternally lost implies an intolerable concession to power outside God. The idea that human self-will could resist divine love even to the uttermost is impossible for Robinson. If even one person were lost, "God would have failed and failed infinitely" (*op. cit.*, p. 118). The key to this position is Robinson's concept of freedom. Like Rahner, he in- sists on the inviolability of human freedom. To clarify his understanding of freedom, he works from the analogy of human love. He speaks of a human love whose power is so great that it leads us to a free acknowl- edgment of its power and to the wonderful moment of total surrender. From this experience, we might be led to think of God's love as a power that draws us in our freedom. It is a power that knows no limits. Surren- der to this love is not a loss of freedom. On the contrary, it is only in such surrender that we discover our true freedom (*op. cit.*, p. 124).

From this basis, Robinson moves to reflect on the Scriptures. At this point, he argues, there can be only one outcome for human life. "All things must be summed up in Christ, because in principle all things already are. Hell is an ultimate impossibility, because *already* there *is* no one outside Christ" (*op. cit.*, p. 130). It remains for each person to choose between life and death. To choose life in Christ is to choose eternal life. To choose against Christ is to choose eternal death. Of this second option Robinson says: " . . . as they choose it and as long as they choose it, it is something that must present itself to them . . . as a choice which is final and irreversible" (*ibid.*). From a human viewpoint, this decision seems definitive, but the truth remains that "love must win" (*op. cit.*, p. 132). "Hell has been harrowed, and none can finally make it their home" (*op. cit.*, p. 133).

The analysis of freedom which provides the basis of this argument is not really opposed to Rahner's view in terms of what it says. It is problematic in that it does not go far enough; it leaves much unsaid. Rahner also understands surrender to the love of God as the place of true human freedom. What Robinson does not discuss and what Rahner refuses to omit is the real possibility that as the human person can close himself or herself to the power of human love, so it is possible to live and die without opening oneself to the love of God.

Hick presents a major statement for the universalist position. He summarizes the non-universalist argument as follows. If we are free, God cannot coerce us. As long as we are free, we can refuse God's invitation. Therefore, as long as we wish to maintain human freedom, it is not possible to say that God will succeed in fulfilling his loving purpose. Hick agrees with Robinson in saying that the mistake of the non-universalists lies in the weak assumption that the only way to universal salvation lies in God's overruling the wayward wills of human beings.

Hick bases his own argument on the idea, drawn from Irenaeus of Lyons, that the human person is created in the image of God. He understands this to mean that we have been created with a God-given capacity to be addressed by and to respond to God. God has no need to coerce us. He has already created us in such a way that our nature, in seeking its own fulfillment, leads us to him. God acts in our history as a divine therapist who removes the blockages that impede our movement to him (*Death and Eternal Life,* pp. 252–54). God, however, does not labor under the limitations of human therapists. He works "in unlimited time, with perfect knowledge, and ultimately controlling instead of being restricted by the environmental factors" (*op. cit.*, p. 254). From this basis, Hick develops his theory of the many stages in this life and in the life beyond whereby the divine therapist works to enable the human person to successfully complete its journey to its ultimate fulfillment with God. Hick summarizes his argument in the following way: "The faith that God has made us for fellowship with himself, and that he so works in his creative power as to enable us to reach that fulfillment, carries with it the faith that in the end all human life will, in traditional theological language, be 'saved'" (*op. cit.*, p. 259). As faith looks to the future, it "becomes a faith in the universal triumph of the divine love" (*ibid.*).

While one cannot deny that this argument has a certain appeal, it labors under weaknesses similar to those in Robinson's argument. Both see the dilemma to be between freedom and coercion. But is this the real point at issue? Is it not rather the question whether a human person can really and finally reject love? Human experience offers evidence of people who seem to be quite capable of doing this, though no one can make any final judgment about such people. Furthermore, the universalist position seems incapable of accepting the idea that in creating the kind of world he has created, God has made himself really dependent on the historical response of his creatures in working out his intention. Neither Robinson nor Hick has offered a convincing solution to the problem of human freedom. It remains an open question whether it is possible to combine freedom with some form of universal salvation.

7
The Dream of Our Future

Among the persistent dreams of the human race is the vision of a time of happiness and peace when the pain and agony of human history will be overcome. The theological term that expresses this dream in religious language is "heaven." How that dream is understood differs in the great religions of the world. For Christian theology the meaning of heaven is determined by the mystery of Christ. In essence, heaven is understood not as a pre-existing place but as the final, fulfilling relation between God and his creation that has been realized in Christ through Jesus' life, death and resurrection, a condition which remains to be realized in the rest of humanity. The "return of Christ" to the Father symbolized by the ascension is the creation of heaven. From this Christological perspective, Christian theology can describe heaven as the new and final dimension of fulfillment for God's creation realized insofar as creation comes home to God. For human beings, this existence with God is essentially an existence with Christ in the presence of the Father. It is communion with the incarnate Word of God and the gathering of humanity into the final body of Christ. The Christian dream is the hope that greater closeness to God will bring greater freedom and fulfillment to all the potential of the human person. How this human future is to be seen in relation to the future of the physical world is a much debated question.

For centuries, Christian theology has emphasized the face-to-face vision of God as the source of our unending happiness. Scripture speaks of our destiny as life. This is not merely biological existence, but a qualitatively deeper and richer way of being. Later theology has seen this life as an intimate participation in the mysterious fullness of the life of

God and has explained it in part by relating it to two functions of the human soul which are basic to the quality of human life: the intellect and the will whereby we know and love the objects of our experience and thus come to live in a qualitatively richer way than the sub-human world. When extended to eschatology, this emphasis on two basic dimensions of human life provides a specific way of interpreting heaven as a symbol for our ultimate fulfillment in eternal life.

It is impossible to give a detailed picture of how a human person can experience a participation in the eternal life of God. Scripture and later theology employ a variety of metaphors (e.g., banquet, wedding feast, beatific vision, etc.) to evoke the awareness of a life that is deeper than that of our present experience. These should not be seen as definitions of heaven. We have no clear knowledge of what heaven will be. At best, we might say that there are moments of human fulfillment in our present life when we seem to break through the limitations of ordinary existence. Such would be profound experiences of love, joy, and unusual creative insights. They are moments when we seem to transcend our normal conditions and savor something richer and deeper. They may well serve as pointers to the reality of heaven.

In his pre-conciliar study of eschatology,[1] Robert Gleason develops his chapter on heaven (pp. 147–70) almost totally in terms of the doctrine of beatific vision. While this model by itself can lead to a strongly individualistic understanding, Gleason takes care to develop his thought in the context of the collective dimension reflected in the metaphor of the body of Christ. This is followed by a sketchy statement about the final destiny of the universe which "depends and receives its orientation from Christ, who draws it toward that definitive state into which He has already entered" (p. 161). Gleason here underscores an ancient Christian insight: "The world in which man lives is man's natural habitat. It shared in man's fall and it must share in his redemption and victory" (p. 163). Gleason thus completes his treatment of heaven with a vision of a cosmos transformed by the power of God in Christ.

Winklhofer also emphasized the model of transformation in speaking of heaven and the destiny of the world in the early 1960's.[2] He sees the power of Christ bringing about a transformation that reaches to the very essence of creation. From the side of humanity, this will mean that the entire universe will become directly accessible to human senses in its entire being, in all its relationships, and in all its intelligible content.

From the side of God, it will mean that the universe will become the completed dwelling place of God. "God lives in it, and it rests in Him who is the end of its being" (*op. cit.,* pp. 243–51).

The major themes of the individual, the collective, and the cosmic will appear in most major treatments up to the present. At times the model of the beatific vision is not strongly emphasized, but some hint of it is found in practically every Roman Catholic author.

In line with the anthropology that is basic to his theological style, Rahner decribes the beatific vision as follows: "It is . . . the direct experience and loving affirmation of God as incomprehensible" (*Encyc.,* p. 80). The mystical tone of Rahner's thought is clear in the following: God's "mystery is not merely the limit of finite cognition, but its ultimate positive ground and final goal, the beatitude of which consists in the ecstatic raising and merging of cognition, without suppressing it, into the bliss of love" (*ibid.*). Here we see Rahner's notion of self-transcendence into the mystery of God as it relates to the individual. But, for Rahner, humanity is so fully social in character that any fulfillment of the individual is incomplete as long as the history of the human race and the world continues. The goal toward which history must move if it is to turn out successfully is the mystery of God-in-Christ. The culmination of the work of creation and redemption is the union of the human race with the triune God. Thus, for Rahner, there is not only the self-transcendence of the individual but the self-transcendence of history as a whole.

For Rahner, our ultimate future—union with the triune God—is a human future. Therefore it requires both the resurrection of the body and a glorified life in a "new heaven and a new earth." This is the final extension of Rahner's anthropology which gives strong emphasis to human nature as "incarnate spirit." If our ultimate fulfillment does not include both spirit and matter, then it is not *our* fulfillment but the fulfillment of a part of our nature. And materiality means that we are inserted into the world and exist always with a relation to the world. The world is the necessary context for our existence as "incarnate spirit." We cannot lose that relation to the world without becoming something other than what our nature presently makes us to be.

Therefore, Christ's second coming, which is the symbol of the end of history as a whole, will mean the glorification of the material creation which is brought to "participation in the perfection of the spirit" (*Invest.*

2, p. 212). Christ's victory will mean not the disappearance of the material world but its final transformation. Those who share in the victory of God's grace at the second coming will be "fully human members of the perfect society which will live with the Incarnate Christ on His glorified earth."[3]

While Rahner's discussion gives little explicit attention to texts of Scripture concerning the end of the world, Anton Vögtle has turned his efforts precisely to that question. A thorough analysis of the scriptural materials leads him to the conclusion that the Christian Scriptures teach nothing definite about the future of the non-human levels of the cosmos.[4] If the scriptural metaphors of a cosmic cataclysm are to be read strictly as metaphors of judgment and not as descriptions of actual cosmic events, what is to be said about positive metaphors such as the new heaven and the new earth? If we follow the same principles of interpretation in both cases, such positive metaphors would seem to refer to the superabundance of salvation rather than to a condition of the physical cosmos. If there is good reason to say that Scripture teaches nothing directly about the future of the physical cosmos, how, then, does it become a theological concern?

How this might happen can be seen in the work of Ratzinger, who takes a sharply critical view of Vögtle's argument. The metaphor which assumes the dominant role in Ratzinger's eschatology is that of a life of interpersonal dialogue. By this he means that eternal life is not derived from some supposed impossibility of dying native to the creature. Rather, it is derived exclusively "from the saving act of one who loves and who has the power to bestow immortality. Man no longer faces the prospect of utter dissolution, because God knows him and loves him. All love desires eternity; God's love not only desires it, but effects it and is it" (*Encyc.*, p. 1451; *Introd.*, p. 271). It is the love of God alone that confers eternity.

Ratzinger's understanding of heaven has an emphatically Christological basis. Heaven is not a place bearing no relation to history. Heaven exists because Jesus Christ has given human existence a place in the being of God. Heaven is primarily a personal relation which remains always marked by its historical origin in the death and resurrection of Christ (*Esch.*, p. 190). As for the rest of humanity, we are in heaven to the degree that we are near Christ. But if heaven is a "being one with Christ," then it necessarily includes a "being with" all those who constitute the body of Christ. Heaven knows no isolation. It is the open communion of saints, and thus the fulfillment of human communion (*Esch.*, p. 191).

But human nature, which is the object of God's saving will, is not to be thought of in isolation from the world in which it exists. Human life includes a wide network of relations with other human beings, with non-human life forms, and with non-living material beings. If human life in its totality is touched by the redemptive work of God in Christ, it is not adequate theologically to limit statements about salvation to some personal center isolated from the network of relations which constitutes this person in its uniqueness. Existence with others is constitutive of human reality and cannot be excluded from whatever further existence may be ours (*Encyc.*, p. 1451). This co-existence includes, first of all, the whole of the human race. When it is extended further to the non-human levels of the world, it becomes clear why Ratzinger argues that concern about the future of the physical world is fundamental to Christian hope (*Esch.*, pp. 157–59).

Schmaus employs both Christological and Trinitarian motifs in speaking of the meaning of eternal life. From a Christological basis, this life is one of union with and conformity to Christ. This becomes explicitly Trinitarian with the idea that Christ leads us into his relation to the Father. "The man who has reached the final fulfillment of existence gives himself to God absolutely, in union with Jesus Christ, the eternal Son of God himself" (*Dogma* 6, p. 263).

The social and cosmic dimensions are emphasized strongly. "Christ's resurrection marks the beginning of heaven; its fullness will be reached with the completion of the total body of Christ as the community of all the members who believe in him" (*op. cit.*, p. 261). Heaven should not be thought of as a state wherein each person who has been saved lives alone with God. On the contrary, each individual lives with a community of sisters and brothers, seeing them in God and seeing God in them (*op. cit.*, p. 268). Schmaus views heaven not as a static condition, but as a movement "from life to life, from joy to joy, from love to love" as we are led to penetrate ever deeper into the mysteries of humanity and of the world in the presence of God (*op. cit.*, p. 272).

Schmaus summarizes his view in the following words. "heaven . . .is nothing other than the future of glorified humanity on a glorified earth, or the glorified creation. All human history is the progress into this absolute future. When it is reached through the coming of man to God through Christ in the Holy Spirit, then the fulfillment will have been attained. . . . The world which comes from God as its sourceless source is a ceaseless motion toward God and into God, and so into itself. . . . The way is full of struggle and confusion, but it is illuminated by the confidence that the goal of human history will be reached: the presence of God, perfect justice and reconciliation, love as the power of a deep, all-embracing brotherhood" (*op. cit.*, p. 273).

Perhaps the most startling ideas on the mystery of eternal life are to be found outside the pale of Catholic theology. For Pannenberg, eternal life will be found in the experience of the unity of our earthly life. Our life in time will be experienced as a non-temporal whole. This means that eternal life has no other content than what we have done in our earthly life. The principal difference between time and eternity consists in the fact that whereas in time we experience ourselves as spread out over past, present, and future, in eternity we will share in God's vision of our earthly life and thus experience our life in its unity.[5] Hick points out that this seems appealing when we are talking about those who have lived full, rich lives, but it becomes obviously problematic in the case of those who have had to endure a poor, stunted existence (*Death and Eternal Life*, p. 225).

In his early writings,[6] Macquarrie describes the future life in terms that reflect both the social and the universalist perspectives. "The end would be a commonwealth of free responsible beings united in love . . . [where] finite existents are preserved in some kind of individual identity," in which "all things are brought to their fulfillment of being," and in which "heaven, purgatory, and hell . . . form a kind of continuum through which the soul may move . . . to the closest union with God" (*op. cit.*, pp. 320–28). Later, in the early 1970's,[7] he gives a strong emphasis to the collective dimension and makes explicit mention of the cosmic. The people of God "will not cease to be until it has led all mankind into the new society of peace, dignity, and freedom" (*Faith*, p. 166). A truly eschatological hope is directed to "the ultimate destiny not only of the people of God but of the whole human race, and, indeed, of the cosmos" (*ibid.*). The scriptural language about a "new heaven and a new earth," a "new creation," and the "resurrection of the dead" implies a "drastic renovation and reconstruction on a cosmic scale" (*op. cit.*, p. 175). In the end, Macquarrie envisions "a community so drastically transformed, so discontinuous with the communities we know now and so transcendent of current utopias, that it could fairly be called eschatological; and yet, as a community recognizably human, personal and fulfilling, it would be in another sense continuous with the communities we know now . . ." (*op. cit.*, p. 177).

More recently, in *Christian Hope*, Macquarrie attempts to develop a possible way of conceiving immortality. Here he suggests that it may be our destiny as individuals "not to live on as immortal souls or to be provided with new bodies, but to be summed up or gathered up in the experience of God . . ." (*op. cit.*, p. 118). At first reading, this sounds very similar to the notion of immortality as "being in the remembrance of God" found in many process theologians. But Macquarrie claims that he does not understand this merely in terms of God's memory. He speaks of an ongoing expansion of communion in which "a past is itself being transformed as God brings about his consummation" (*op. cit.*, p. 120). This does not mean that he makes the past "not to have happened." But "the value of these facts can be changed and often is changed" (*ibid.*). This view labors under the same problem as that of process theology. The memory of self is not the same as the self. It is hard to see anything like a subjective immortality for the human person in reflections that speak of God's memory of us.

If these reflections on heaven and eternal life seem somewhat strange and far removed from Christian faith, we need to remind ourselves that the purpose of such reflections is simply to show that the Christian hope for the future of humanity and the world does not have to be seen as a childish illusion or as an irresponsible refusal to face human life with all its dark moments. To speak of eternal life is not a piece of nonsense lacking any clear rational support. We are, in fact, dealing with the outer reaches of human hope. If it is difficult to imagine what those outer reaches might be like, it is the task of theology to use whatever resources are available to shed light on the issue. In the final analysis, the Christian need be committed to no specific model of eschatological speculation. Ultimately Christian hope rests not on a specific style of theology but on the conviction "that if God is indeed the God of love revealed in Jesus Christ, then death will not wipe out his care for the persons he has created" (*op. cit.*, p. 127).

Conclusion

The kingdom of God, which was the central concern of the preaching of Jesus, symbolizes the final relation between God and his world. It is a symbol that evokes the sense of a collective state of salvation beyond death where the power of God's creative, life-giving love will not be contravened. In terms of the Christian Scriptures, this is a future community of human beings with God that transcends national and political categories. The transcendental rule of God cannot be identified totally with any future that we can plan and build by ourselves. It cannot be identified with any specific institution or event within the world.

This does not mean, however, that the coming of the kingdom is unrelated to the events of history. The Christian eschatological attitude is one of vigilant, hopeful expectation. It looks forward not to an emptiness but to an ultimate fullness of life in a future that transcends death and history. To speak in the metaphor of Exodus, we can say that Christians are called to see life as a going-forth. But this going-forth is not a Platonic flight from the world. It is, rather, a going-forth together with the world to fulfillment in the presence of God.

Christian hope involves the conviction that the world will be brought to fulfillment with humanity. Christian tradition has no binding understanding as to *how* humanity and the world will be related, or *how* this fulfillment will be brought about. While there is no information about the end to guide us in our practical conduct as Christians, the attitude of Jesus remains a source of insight and hope for believers. He remains ever the model of radical trust in the life-giving love of God and of the authentic response to God. From his life we may conclude that humanity alone can never reach its true fulfillment from out of its own resources. And God cannot bring about this fulfillment without an ap-

67

propriate human response to his love. We do not know how God acts in and through human actions, but we can be sure that without human response, God's action does not come to term.

Hope is an openness to the future. At one level, it is a passive attitude. Just as we are given existence and thus are first passive recipients of the gift of life, so we are ultimately given our future as a pure gift of God's grace. But the existence that we receive evokes an active response in us. We must actively live our history. What we make of ourselves in history is the crucial condition for the final gift of God to his creatures. Our ultimate fulfillment is found in a relationship with God. However, the depth and richness of that relationship is conditioned by the kind of persons we have become in history.

Therefore, at a second level, hope is active. It is not a fatalistic capitulation to an inevitable flow of history. What we do with our lives makes a difference for the kingdom of God. Our hope in the future kingdom should alert us to the many cheap substitutes offered us in the course of history, substitutes that never correspond to the depth of human hope. It should generate within us an active concern about all those conditions in human life and society that impede the coming of God's kingdom. Hope, therefore, is not mere passive waiting. It is also active, co-creative responsibility for the future of the world and of humanity.

Though it has no concrete image of the future, and though it may not even clearly see progress in history, Christian hope works actively in the service of God and of humanity, striving to create within history the condition for the realization of the kingdom by building the earth and contributing to the enrichment of human life and love. Hope does this in spite of the spectre of death, leading a life between the cross and resurrection—a life that is both worldly and eschatological, lived under the sign of the cross and in the power of the Spirit.

Notes

Chapter 1

1. *Der Römerbrief* (Munich, 1922), p. 486.
2. *Op. cit.*, p. 298.
3. "Eschatologie," in *Fragen der Theologie Heute*, ed. J. Feiner *et al.* (Einsiedeln, 1958), pp. 403–21: English tr.: "Eschatology," in *Theology Today* I (Milwaukee, 1964), pp. 222–44.
4. Johannes Weiss, *Die Predigt Jesu vom Reiche Gottes* (Göttingen, 1900²).
5. Albert Schweitzer, *The Quest of the Historical Jesus* (London, 1922²).
6. C.H. Dodd, *The Parables of the Kingdom* (London, 1941).
7. Rudolf Bultmann, *History and Eschatology* (Edinburgh, 1957).
8. Oscar Cullmann, *Christ and Time* (Philadelphia, 1964); *Salvation in History* (London, 1967).
9. Jürgen Moltmann, *Theology of Hope* (New York, 1967).
10. Johannes B. Metz, *Theology of the World* (New York, 1969).
11. Jürgen Moltmann, *The Crucified God* (New York, 1974).
12. "The Future in the Memory of Suffering," in *Concilium* 76 (1972), pp. 9–25, esp. p. 13.
13. *Naherwartung Auferstehung Unsterblichkeit. Quaestiones Disputatae*, Vol. 71 (Freiburg, 1975).
14. Johann Auer and Joseph Ratzinger, *Kleine Katholische Dogmatik*, Vol. 9 (Regensburg, 1977).
15. *Hoffnung auf Vollendung: Aufriss der Eschatologie. Quaestiones Disputatae*, Vol. 90 (Freiburg, 1980).

16. Leonardo Boff, *Jesus Christ Liberator* (Maryknoll, 1978); Gustavo Gutiérrez, *A Theology of Liberation* (Maryknoll, 1973); Juan Luis Segundo, *Liberation Theology* (Maryknoll, 1976); Jon Sobrino, *Christology at the Crossroads* (Maryknoll, 1978); Segundo Galilea, *Following Jesus* (Maryknoll, 1981).

Chapter 2

1. Yves Congar, "Fins derniers," in *Revue de Sciences Philosophiques et Théologiques* 33 (1949), pp. 463–84; Hans Urs von Balthasar, *op. cit.*

2. Jean Daniélou, "Christologie et Eschatologie," in *Das Konzil von Chalkedon*, III (Würzburg, 1954), pp. 269–86.

3. Carl E. Braaten, *History and Hermeneutics. New Directions in Theology Today*, Vol. 2 (Philadelphia, 1966), pp. 178–79.

4. Karl Rahner, "The Hermeneutics of Eschatological Assertions," in *Theological Investigations* 4 (London, 1966), pp. 323–46.

5. *Mysterium Salutis: Grundriss heilsgeschichtlicher Dogmatik*, Vol. 5: *Zwischenzeit und Vollendung der Heilsgeschichte*, (Einsiedeln, 1976), p. 645.

6. Edward Schillebeeckx, "The Interpretation of Eschatology," in *Concilium* 41 (1969), pp. 42–56; *The Understanding of Faith: Interpretation and Criticism* (New York, 1974) pp. 1–13.

7. "The Interpretation of Eschatology," p. 53.

8. *Ibid.*

9. Ernst Bloch, *Prinzip Hoffnung* (Frankfurt, 1959).

10. John Macquarrie, *Christian Hope* (New York, 1978).

11. Carl E. Braaten, "Toward a Theology of Hope, in: *New Theology*, #5, ed. Marty & Peerman (New York/London, 1968) pp. 90–111.

Chapter 4 (no notes in chapter three)

1. Wolfhart Pannenberg, *Theology and the Kingdom of God* (Philadelphia, 1969), p. 74.

2. *Op. cit.*, p. 89.

3. *Inv.*, 10, pp. 260–72.

4. Johannes B. Metz, *Faith in History and Society* (New York, 1980), p. 109.

5. J.A.T. Robinson, *In the End God* (London/New York, 1968), p. 70.

6. *Catholic Biblical Quarterly* 12 (1950), pp. 243–47.

7. *Handbuch Theologischer Grundbegriffe,* Vol. 1 (Munich, 1962), p. 335.

8. *Op. cit.,* p. 333.

9. *Das Neue Testament und die Zukunft des Kosmos* (Düsseldorf, 1970).

10. *Auferstehung der Toten* (Essen, 1969), p. 410.

11. *Revelation as History* (Toronto, 1968), p. 133.

Chapter 5

1. A. Winklhofer, *The Coming of His Kingdom* (New York, 1963), p. 164.

2. *Dictionary of the Bible* (Milwaukee, 1965), p. 640.

3. *The Resurrection* (New York, 1960).

4. *The Last Things* (New York, 1954).

5. *And the Life Everlasting* (Oxford, 1934, 1960).

6. G. Greshake, G. Lohfink, *Naherwartung Auferstehung Unsterblichkeit* (Freiburg, 1975); L. Boros, "Has Life a Meaning?" in *Concilium* 60 (1970), pp. 11–20; *Mysterium Salutis* 5 (Benziger, 1976), pp. 882ff.

7. G. McCool, *Rahner Reader* (New York, 1975) p. 358.

Chapter 6

1. K. Rahner and H. Vorgrimler, *Theological Dictionary* (New York, 1981²), p. 426.

2. *Hoffnung auf Vollendung,* p. 161.

3. *Lexikon für Theologie und Kirche* 5, col. 448.

4. *We Are Future* (New York, 1973) p. 155.

Chapter 7

1. *The World To Come* (New York, 1958).

2. *The Coming of His Kingdom* (New York, 1963).

3. G. McCool, *Rahner Reader,* p. 358.

4. *Das Neue Testament . . .,* p. 233.

5. *What Is Man?* (Philadelphia, 1972), pp. 49–50, 80.

6. *Principles of Christian Theology* (New York, 1966).

7. *The Faith of the People of God* (New York, 1972).

Bibliography

1. German Works

Greshake, Gisbert; Lohfink, Gerhard, *Naherwartung Auferstehung Unsterblichkeit. Quaestiones Disputatae,* 71. Herder, Freiburg, 1975.

Ratzinger, Joseph Cardinal, *Eschatologie: Tod und Ewiges Leben. Kleine Katholische Dogmatik,* IX. Pustet, Regensburg, 1977.

Vorgrimler, Herbert, *Hoffnung auf Vollendung. Aufriss der Eschatologie. Quaestiones Disputatae,* 90. Herder, Freiburg, 1980.

2. English Works

Durrwell, F.X., *The Resurrection.* tr. R. Sheed. Sheed & Ward, N.Y., 1960.

Greshake, Gisbert, "Toward a Theology of Dying," in *Concilium* 94 (1974) pp. 80–98.

Hick, John, *Death and Eternal Life.* Harper & Row, N.Y., 1976.

Lohfink, Gerhard, *Is Death the Final Word?* Franciscan Herald Press, Chicago, 1977.

Macquarrie, John, *Christian Hope.* Seabury Press, N.Y., 1978.

Morse, Christopher, *The Logic of Promise in Moltmann's Theology.* Fortress Press, Philadelphia, 1979.

Rahner, Karl, *On the Theology of Death.* Herder & Herder, N.Y., 1961.

————, "The Hermeneutics of Eschatological Assertions," in *Theological Investigations* 4, Darton, Longman, & Todd, London, 1966, pp. 323–346.

Robinson, J.A.T., *In the End God*. Fontana, London; Harper & Row, N.Y., 1968.

Schillebeeckx, Edward, "The Interpretation of Eschatology," in *Concilium* 41. Paulist Press, N.Y., 1969, pp. 42–56.

————, *The Understanding of Faith. Interpretation and Criticism.* Seabury, N.Y., 1974.

Schmaus, Michael, *Dogma 6: Justification and the Last Things*. Sheed & Ward, London, Kansas City, 1977.

Travis, Stephen H., *Christian Hope and the Future of Man*. Inter-Varsity Press, Leicester, England, 1980.

Von Balthasar, Hans Urs, "Eschatology," in *Theology Today* I, ed. J. Feiner, *et al*. Bruce, Milwaukee, 1964, pp. 222–244.

Winklhofer, Alois, *The Coming of His Kingdom*. Herder & Herder, N.Y., 1963.